PAUL'S VISION
for the
TEACHING CHURCH

PAUL'S VISION
for the
TEACHING CHURCH

David L. Bartlett

Judson Press® Valley Forge

LAKE
VIEW
BOOKS

Lake View Books are books of outstanding merit and broad interest which originated at the American Baptist Assembly, Green Lake, Wisconsin. The material on which this book is based was presented under the Boardman Lectureship at Green Lake.

Library of Congress Cataloging in Publication Data

Bartlett, David Lyon, 1941—
    Paul's vision for the teaching church.

    Revision and expansion of lectures given at the Learning One '76 Conference at the American Baptist Assembly, Green Lake, Wis.
    Bibliography: pp. 137-138.
    1. Church—Teaching office—Biblical teaching—
Addresses, essays, lectures.   2. Bible.   N. T.
Epistles of Paul—Theology—Addresses, essays, lectures.
I. Title.
BS2655.C5B37   261.1   77-1106
ISBN 0-8170-0738-5

For all those with whom
I worked and worshiped
at University Baptist Church, Minneapolis

"Love never ends."

Acknowledgments

This book is a revision and expansion of the lectures I gave at the Learning One '76 conference at the American Baptist Assembly, Green Lake, Wisconsin. I am grateful to Richard Sammer and Bud Carroll of the Board of Educational Ministries of the American Baptist Churches, who have encouraged me in this project. I am grateful to Judson Press for choosing this book as the Boardman Lectures for 1976 and to Harold Twiss and Phyllis Frantz for their advice and editorial skills.

I express my thanks to Cathy Fairfield and to my sister, Marion Van Arsdell, for reading parts of the typescript and making helpful suggestions and to Cathy Fairfield for typing the entire text. Jerry Nord graciously provided space for me to finish writing. I also want to thank my research assistant Robert Fowler for his work in preparing the Index.

The members of my class on Paul's theology, at the University of Chicago in spring, 1976, greatly expanded my understanding of Paul.

I have two special debts of gratitude: first, to all those who participated in Learning One '76, who gave me crucial support and suggestions for this book; second, to the members of the Hyde Park Union Church in Chicago, who encourage me to study, teach, and write and who are my teachers.

Contents

Introduction

This book is a study of the implications of Paul's theology for our understanding of the teaching church. In many ways it seems an unlikely project since Paul doesn't have much to say about "*the* church" and Paul doesn't have much to say about teaching.

Paul doesn't have much to say about *the* church because he is always concerned with this church or that church. There is one church—the church at Philippi—with which he's very happy. There are other churches—the churches in Galatia—with which he's very unhappy. About the rest of his churches he has mixed feelings. He writes to specific churches out of a mixture of pride and anguish. His concern is not for any general doctrine of the church; his concern is for reminding the Corinthians of the faith which he preached, or for comforting the Thessalonians in their distress. In order to get any doctrine of the church from Paul, we need to abstract that doctrine from the concrete, specific interests which inform his letters.

Furthermore, Paul has surprisingly little to say about teaching, at least in the most narrow sense. It is remarkable how seldom the words "teach" or "teaching" appear in his letters. Certainly Paul has little concern for the kinds of questions we usually raise about the church's teaching ministry. He is not worried about curriculum, nor about the structure of the church school, nor about recruiting church school teachers, nor about the membership of the board of Christian education.

The reason that Paul isn't concerned with the kinds of educational structures which concern us is that he doesn't think there is time for those kinds of structures. He thinks that in Jesus Christ the kingdom of God has already begun to come and that in Jesus Christ the kingdom of God will soon come in its fullness. Therefore, there is really not time to choose a curriculum, or to make long-range plans for the church school, or to worry about the membership of the board of education.

Yet what seems to be odd about using Paul as a guide to the church's teaching ministry may actually prove helpful to us.

To be sure, Paul isn't much worried about the church in general, but most of the time neither are we. We are worried about the concrete needs and hopes of this church or that church: our church in Des Moines or Ashtabula or Chicago. We come to a study like this one with specific questions, specific needs. The very fact that Paul could speak to a variety of specific problems and needs may be a help to us as we look at the diversity of our own churches. We may find that one word of Paul's speaks to us with great power, while another seems less pertinent. We may discover that Paul's major theological concerns have a different application to our church than they do to the church at Rome or Philippi. We are free to be as specific and as diverse as Paul's letters are.

To be sure, Paul doesn't write about teaching in traditional ways, but maybe that is healthy for us. He may remind us that there are some prior questions which we need to ask before we can move on to questions of curriculum and structure. He may cause us to ask questions like: What is the church? Is the church school just like any other kind of school, or does it have a special function? Is the church school the only means by which the church teaches?

Why do we teach? Is it to pass on information, or to evoke ethical commitment, or to entice people to new life?

How do we teach? Are there any methods which are especially appropriate to the church?

What do we teach? Do we teach doctrines, or stories, or ways to respond to personal problems, or even a whole new life?

There is at least one place where Paul talks explicitly about his understanding of teaching.

But thanks be to God, that you who were once slaves of sin have become obedient from the heart to the standard of teaching to which you were committed, and, having been set free from sin, have become slaves of righteousness (Romans 6:17-18).

Already this gives us some clues to Paul's understanding of the church's teaching ministry. It suggests that, for Paul, teaching is not just a matter of passing on information but of evoking faithful obedience. It suggests that, for Paul, the church's teaching is not just a matter of giving people new ideas but a matter of giving them new life, of setting them free from sin, and of putting them in a right relationship to God and to other people.

I hope that these chapters will help us appreciate Paul's basic vision of the church and its ministry. I hope that that vision will enable our churches to move toward that kind of teaching which evokes faithful obedience and frees people for a new and richer life.

1

What Is the Church Which Teaches? The Community of the New Age

There is a deeply felt need among many within the church to come to a richer vision of the church's teaching ministry. Too often the church's educational program has been seen as an auxiliary to the "main work" of the church. At worst, "Christian education" has been a code word for baby-sitting provided during the morning worship; at best, Christian education has been the responsibility of one board whose concerns are confined to one segment of the church community—children—and to one portion of the week—Sunday between 9:45 A.M. and 12 noon. Our style of education has sometimes been dictated by an overzealous devotion to the pedagogical techniques of our forebears in the faith, and at other times it has been shifted by every new wind that blows from the general direction of popular psychology or "relevant" educational theory.

Surely we have much to learn from psychologists and educators about our role as a teaching church. However, surely the place to begin any search for greater self-understanding is with the primary source for our self-understanding: the biblical Word.

My own theological convictions about the significance of Christ, the shape of the Christian life, and the meaning of the Christian community have been mostly shaped by the writings of the apostle

Paul. It is my belief that a study of Paul's writings can provide some essential guidelines for us as we seek to understand the teaching ministry of the church.

Before we can understand the church's role as teacher, however, we need to understand what Paul thinks the church itself is. To be sure, Paul is less concerned with writing a doctrine of *the* church than with writing comfort and advice to this or that particular church. Nevertheless, some themes and concerns run throughout Paul's letters. A careful reading of those letters allows us to discover what Paul thinks makes the church the church. This is crucial for our discussion of the teaching church because if we're not really being the church, there's not much point in our teaching. If we are really being the church, that fact is found to affect both what we teach and how we teach. We will suggest in this chapter that for Paul the church is the community of the New Age. In order to understand that, we need first to understand some of the assumptions which Paul shared in common with many first-century Jews.

The Jewish Hope for the Age to Come

In the last two centuries before the birth of Christ, history went particularly badly for the Jewish people. In the sixth and fifth centuries before Christ the people of Judea began to return to their land after their exile in Babylon. However, they never regained the power or stability of their earlier regimes—particularly the regimes of David and Solomon, which they recalled with longing. From the time of Alexander the Great in the late fourth century B.C. Palestine was largely under foreign rule. The situation became particularly bad during the second century before Christ when Palestine was under the control of Seleucid (Persian) rulers. The most tyrannical of the Seleucid kings was Antiochus Epiphanes (who reigned 175–163 B.C.). Antiochus began his reign by encouraging Jews to give up their Jewish practices and become more' and more cosmopolitan and Greek. By the end of his reign he had virtually outlawed the practice of the Jewish faith and—outrageously—had desecrated the temple by erecting there an altar to Zeus.

Faithful Jews were appalled and rallied behind the leadership of Mattathias and, after his death, his son, Judas Maccabaeus. Judas and his followers succeeded in freeing Judea from the rule of the Seleucids after a long struggle. However, the freedom of Palestine was short-lived. The successors to the original Maccabees fought among themselves for power until finally Rome stepped in; and in 63 B.C., Palestine became part of the Roman Empire.[1]

The apparent disaster of their history provided a profound theological dilemma for faithful Jews. The belief which they had cherished, at least from the time of the Davidic kingdom, was that God was active in their history. God was active in their history providing both judgment and blessing, to be sure; but always the final word was blessing. Now the final word seemed to be judgment or— worse yet—inexplicable oppression and misery.

Since God no longer seemed to be acting in history, faithful Jews began to look for God *beyond* history. They began to hope that God would redeem the world at the end of history, and they began to hope that the end of history would come soon.

This hope emerged in Jewish literature at least as early as the Book of Daniel, written during the time of Antiochus Epiphanes in the second century B.C. The hope pervaded a good deal of what we call the "intertestamental literature"—books like First Enoch and the Testament of the Twelve Patriarchs (whose dating is sometimes disputed). The literature which stresses the hope for God to redeem history at the end of history is called "apocalyptic literature." *Apokalypsis* is the Greek word for "revelation," and in Greek the last book of the Bible—Revelation—is called *Apokalypsis*. The book of Revelation is permeated with the hope for God's saving activity at the end of history.

By the time of Jesus and Paul, apocalyptic literature was widespread in Palestine and apocalyptic hope even more so. In addition to the apocalyptic books we have mentioned, there is clear evidence in early rabbinic writings that many Jews who were closely attached to the synagogues and schools believed that God would soon bring a new age and an end to the present painful world order. The Zealots believed, if not in a brand-new world, at least in a much better history brought about by their own rebellious action against the Roman occupation. The Qumran community (that community which preserved the Dead Sea Scrolls) was a community which lived a monastic existence as it awaited the final war between faithful Jews and Romans and their sympathizers. At the end of that war the Qumran community believed that God would intervene and redeem history for the faithful.

Sometimes particular figures were expected to emerge at the end of time. Some expected Elijah; some expected a new Moses; some expected a new king who would be as great as David. The word "messiah" means "anointed one." Kings were anointed, and those who were looking for a messiah were apparently looking for someone who would be a king like David. (Messianic expectations were not always that consistent; the people in Qumran apparently expected a "messiah" who would be a priest as well.)

Also in some of the literature, especially Daniel and First Enoch (and some of the material picked up in our Gospels), there is speculation about a coming "son of man"—apparently a heavenly figure who will come at the end of time on clouds of glory.[2]

Most important—for us at least—there is no question that Jesus himself shared a kind of apocalyptic view. His preaching centered on the use of a particular symbol—the symbol of the kingdom of God.[3] This symbol of the kingdom of God had nuances which can only be called apocalyptic. Jesus' preaching, particularly his parables, called attention to the age which was coming, an age in which God would establish God's kingly rule over the whole creation. However, there was a unique feature to Jesus' preaching. Jesus maintained that the kingdom of God was already impinging, breaking in on history. More than that, Jesus claimed that the kingdom of God was impinging on history precisely in Jesus himself. Jesus' words not only mentioned the kingdom, but they announced it as well: "Here it is!" Jesus' miracles, especially his exorcisms of demons, weren't just sensational crowd-grabbers; they were signs of the kingdom. They, too, pointed to the kingdom; indeed they acted out the kingdom. Jesus' willingness to eat meals with all the most undesirable elements of society was itself a part of that kingdom where all God's people were brought together, not by their achievements, but by the mercy of God. For Jesus the Age to Come was already coming. It was not altogether present; almost certainly there was a fuller consummation to be expected. However, the Age to Come had begun, and it had begun in the person of Jesus himself.[4]

The Christian church, in a variety of ways, laid hold on Jesus' claim that the kingdom was breaking in and it was happening in the life and ministry of Jesus himself. The church further had to deal with two factors which Jesus did not deal with explicitly in his own teaching.

The church had to deal with the cross. If Jesus was really the one in whom the kingdom was breaking in (as the church claimed, if Jesus was really the Messiah), how could this terrible thing happen to him?

It was not simply that he died prematurely or tragically. It was that he died an outcast, a criminal, a laughingstock. Once again it would seem that God had deserted history. The very one who was to bring the kingdom was executed as an outlaw.

Further, the church had to deal with the resurrection. Here was a remarkable new phenomenon. This Jesus had been raised from the dead, but the one who had been raised from the dead was still the crucified one. His ministry had been vindicated, but he had still been vindicated as the one who had died outrageously. He had been raised from the dead, but what did that mean for other people? Was his resurrection the beginning of the consummation of the Age to Come? Would the risen Lord soon come again? When? How? These were the questions with which the early church was deeply concerned.

These, of course, were questions which grew out of that hope which Christians continued to share with their Jewish brothers and sisters: the hope for the Age to Come. Christians, however, had a new belief. They believed that in the person of Jesus the Age to Come had already made inroads into history. They believed—most astonishingly—that the crucified outlaw had been acknowledged by God to be that expected one who would bring the kingdom, who would bring a gracious end to human history.

Paul and the Hope for the Age to Come

We know that Paul had been a good Jew because he tells us so:

> . . . . If any other man thinks he has reason for confidence in the flesh, I have more: circumcised on the eighth day, of the people of Israel, of the tribe of Benjamin, a Hebrew born of Hebrews; as to the law a Pharisee (Philippians 3:4-5).

Paul does not here explicitly speak of sharing the common Jewish expectation of the Age to Come, but he does claim to be a Pharisee. The Pharisaic party was that party in Palestine which believed in the resurrection of the dead. In this sense, at least, they were an apocalyptic party; and we can infer that Paul had shared their hope for God's gracious activity beyond history.[5]

Whatever Paul's belief about the Age to Come, he clearly had not been persuaded by the Christian claim that the Age to Come had already begun to come in Jesus, who was the expected One. Indeed, Paul continues the summary of his activity as a Jew with these words: "As to zeal [I was] a persecutor of the church" (Philippians 3:6a).

We don't know the particular reasons for Paul's zealous

opposition to the Christians. We can guess that he may have found particularly offensive the claim that one who was crucifed as an outlaw could have been the Promised One, the one who would bring God's rule to earth. The fact that Paul later recognized the cross as a major stumbling block to others' faith may indicate that it had been a major stumbling block to his faith as well. (See 1 Corinthians 1:18, 23.)

Then Paul underwent an astonishing change. He became not only a Christian but an apostle also. He describes the change in this way:

> I did not receive the gospel from man, nor was I taught it, but I received it through a revelation of Jesus Christ. For you've heard of my previous conduct in Judaism, how I eagerly persecuted the church of God and tried to destroy it; and I advanced in Judaism beyond many of my own age among my people, so extremely zealous was I for the traditions of my fathers. But when he who had set me apart before I was born, and had called me through his grace, was pleased to reveal his Son through [Greek, "in"] me, in order that I might preach him among the Gentiles, I did not confer with flesh and blood (Galatians 1:12-16, with some translation emendations by the author).

A remarkable reversal took place for Paul. He changed, of course, from a non-Christian Jew to a Jewish Christian. He changed from a persecutor of the church to an apostle and a founder of churches.

More than that, however (and we cannot emphasize this too strongly), the *world* had changed. History had changed. Paul realized that he lived in a totally different age from the one he had thought. He had thought he lived in the Old Age, the age which still awaited God's rule, which still awaited the Promised One. He discovered to his own immense astonishment that he lived in a New Age. God's rule was *already* impinging upon history. The Promised One had *already* come. Paul's awakening was a little like Rip Van Winkle's waking up after twenty years to discover that he was a citizen in a new nation. But Paul's awakening was instantaneous, and he woke up to discover that he was a citizen of a brand-new world. In Second Corinthians, Paul writes of the change in this way: "If anyone is in Christ, *there is a new creation!* The old has passed away, behold, the new has come" (2 Corinthians 5:17, emended by the author). (The Revised Standard Version says, "If any one is in Christ, *he* is a new creation" [author's italics], but the context makes my translation more likely.) Paul here insists that for him—for all Christians—there is a new creation day.

The whole world is made over again. The Age to Come has come and is coming.

Paul takes up a good deal of his correspondence trying to explain to his readers how it is that for Christians there is a new creation. Throughout this book we shall look at the various arguments Paul uses, but certainly this passage from Second Corinthians provides one central statement of Paul's claim. Here is the whole passage:

> From now on, therefore, we regard no one from a human point of view [literally, "according to the flesh"]; even though we once regarded Christ from a human point of view, we regard him thus no longer. Therefore, if any one is in Christ, there is a new creation; the old has passed away, behold, the new has come. All this is from God, who through Christ reconciled us to himself and gave us the ministry of reconciliation; that is, God was in Christ reconciling the world to himself, not counting their trespasses against them, and entrusting to us the ministry of reconciliation (2 Corinthians 5:16-19, with some emendations by the author).

In this brief passage Paul shows why he believes that in the cross of Christ God has brought about a new creation. Every sentence of the passage shows one way in which Paul believes that God has reversed human expectations and has initiated the Age to Come.

(1) "From now on, therefore, we regard no one from a human point of view [according to the flesh]; even though we once regarded Christ from a human point of view [according to the flesh], we regard him thus no longer." In the Old Age, i.e., the age which has passed away, Paul and everybody else looked at things "according to the flesh," from "a human point of view." In the Old Age Paul assumed that what counted were human standards—power, prestige, success. Therefore, he was convinced that Jesus was either a great fraud or a great failure. Though Jesus and his followers had claimed that Jesus was bringing the Age to Come, that belief was apparently rendered ridiculous by the crucifixion. From a human point of view the crucifixion was a disgrace, and the crucified was an outlaw and a fool.

When Paul says, "We regard him thus no longer," he speaks of the radical shift in his own thinking. He now realizes that the crucifixion was not a disgrace but the means of God's grace; he realizes that though the crucified One was an outlaw and a fool by human standards, he was also God's Messiah and the Lord of the New Age.

(2) "All this is from God, who through Christ reconciled us to himself . . . that is, God was in Christ reconciling the world to

himself." You will remember that the Jewish people believed that the Old Age, the age in which they lived, was marked by God's inactivity. God seemed to have departed from history and left people to their own devices or to the sway of malicious powers. Paul believes that the New Age has come precisely because the God who seemed to be absent is now strikingly, mercifully present in human history. That's what reconciliation means—that God's absence is turned to presence. The gap between people and God is bridged absolutely and forever.

Most remarkably, that reconciliation takes place in the crucified One. Most remarkably, it is in Christ that the apparently absent God becomes present. Most remarkably, it is in Christ that the gap between people and God is bridged absolutely and forever. The New Age has come precisely because people have been "reconciled to God." That reconciliation, that vast change in the whole history of the world, has a date and a place. The date is Good Friday; the place is Calvary.

(3) "Not counting their trespasses against them." Another mark of the Old Age was that it was an age of sin and judgment. People tried to appease the distant God by faithfully keeping the law. Yet, time and again they failed to keep that law and feared that when the New Age came, when God was present fully among them, they would face God's awful wrath. Paul claims that the New Age has come; God is present. But God is present in mercy more than in wrath. God does not count the trespasses of the world against them.

(4) "And entrusting to us the ministry of reconciliation." Paul refers first of all here to himself. The persecutor who had been an agent of destruction has become a minister of reconciliation. Because there is a new world, Paul lives in that world as a new kind of person. Paul also refers to the whole community of Christians. The job of Christians is to live as faithful citizens of the New Age. The job of Christians is to proclaim and act out the reconciliation which has come in Jesus Christ. The job of Christians is to proclaim and act out the presence of God in a gracious new world.

Paul's radical belief that God was in Christ makes it possible for him to say: "If anyone is in Christ, there is a new creation. The old has passed away. Behold, the new has come."

At this point we need to add a cautionary note. While Paul affirms with remarkable fervor that in the cross and resurrection of Christ the New Age has come, there is also another element to his understanding of history. He also believes that the *fullness* of the New

Age is yet to come. We shall discuss the implications of this belief at greater length later, but here we will cite two instances of Paul's reminder that while the kingdom has come, the fullness of the kingdom is yet to come.

> Not that I have already obtained this [presumably, resurrection] or am already perfect; but I press on to make it my own, because Christ Jesus has made me his own (Philippians 3:12).

> For now we see in a mirror dimly, but then face to face. Now I know in part; then I shall understand fully, even as I have been fully understood (1 Corinthians 13:12).

This cautionary note will be useful as we look at the church as the community of the New Age. If we thought only of the church as that community which lives in the New Age of God's gracious rule, we might get discouraged when we look at our churches, which are often noticeably dragging their feet en route to the kingdom. We may be heartened to discover that Paul's churches also entered the kingdom reluctantly and had useful exhortations for them and for us as well.

The Church as the Community of the New Age

For Paul the church is that community of people who know that the New Age has come in Jesus Christ and who live as citizens of that New Age. For anyone who is in Christ, there is a new creation. (See 2 Corinthians 5:17.) For Paul those who are "in Christ" are those who are in the church. Church people, therefore, are those who know that "the old has passed away, behold, the new has come" (2 Corinthians 5:17b). Because church people are citizens of the New Age, many of the traditional marks of other institutions and communities don't apply to the church. Other institutions and communities are associated with the Old Age which is passing away. The New Age requires a new kind of community. There are at least three distinctive characteristics of this new community, the church. For Paul the church is a community without credentials; it is a community without distinctions; and it is a community without end. We shall look at each of these marks of the new community to see what Paul is saying about the nature of the church.

The Community Without Credentials

According to Paul, the distinguishing mark of the Old Age (which he called the age of the flesh) was that everyone was constantly trying to prove his or her credentials. Everyone was always trying to prove that his or her life was worthwhile and worth living. Everyone was always trying to flaunt his or her status. Most remarkably, everyone was always trying to flaunt his or her status in the eyes of God.

In the Old Age some people tried to prove their credentials by their godliness. The people Paul was angry at when he wrote the letter to the Galatians were apparently people who thought that they could prove their credentials by showing how godly they were.

For Paul's Galatian opponents, showing how godly they were meant obeying at least some of the rules of the Jewish law. They were trying to persuade the Galatian Christians that if they were to win God's favor, they must take upon themselves at least some of the obligations of the Jewish law. So they were urging the Galatian men to be circumcised, as the law required; and apparently they were urging all the Galatian people to observe the various holidays of the Jewish calendar, as the law required. These were ways of showing everyone (including God) how godly they were. These were ways of winning God's favor. (See Galatians 4:10; 5:2.)

When Paul wrote to the Romans, he suggested that the problem with the people of Israel over the years was that they, too, tried to show their credentials before God. At least Paul, as one Jew, knew that he had tried to win God's favor by his godliness. Again, circumcision was a sign for the Jews of their godliness (Romans 2:25-29).

Apparently the Galatians and some Jews had a kind of "Boy Scout" view of their relationship to God. They thought that if one worked hard enough, one got spiritual "merit badges." Males could get a merit badge for being circumcised. Everyone could get a merit badge for observing festivals or for keeping the sabbath. On Judgment Day you would appear before the throne of God wearing your merit badge sash. Spiritual Eagle Scouts would receive mercy; spiritual Tenderfeet could expect only judgment.[6]

The stress on showing one's credentials, the stress on godliness, however, was a mark of the Old Age. Paul tells us that there are two advantages of being a citizen of the New Age, two advantages of being in the church.

The first advantage is that you know you *can't* win God's favor by your godliness. That is Paul's great insight into the hazards of life in the Old Age. If you try to win God's favor by your godliness, you may seek desperately to obey all the commands of the law and discover that you're still stuck with your selfishness. Then you fall into despair; you don't believe God *can* help you. Or if you try to win God's favor by your godliness, you may discover that you're doing very well indeed. Then you fall into pride; you don't believe God *needs* to help you. That pride is the most profound kind of sin. So Paul writes: "For no human being will be justified in [God's] sight by works of the law, since through the law comes knowledge of sin" (Romans 3:20).

However, the second advantage of being a citizen of the New Age, a church person, is that you know you *don't have to* win God's favor by your godliness. In Romans Paul speaks in yet another way of the great reversal in human history, the new creation: "While we were still weak, at the right time Christ died for the ungodly" (Romans 5:6). The reason that Christians don't have to win God's favor by their godliness is that God has already given them God's favor in Jesus Christ. There are some things which our supposed godliness might earn. It might earn us the commendation of other people. It might earn us a sense of our own spiritual well-being. It might earn us a certain amount of fame and publicity. But our godliness cannot possibly earn us the great gift which Christ has given us. Our godliness cannot possibly earn the gift of Christ's death on the cross. That kind of gift is sheer gift—unearned, undeserved, beyond credentials, and beyond godliness: "Why, one will hardly die for a righteous man—though perhaps for a good man one will dare even to die. But God shows his love for us in that while we were yet sinners Christ died for us" (Romans 5:7-8).

Furthermore, our very attempt to be godly may get in the way of our recognizing God's favor when we see it. The attempt to be godly may get in the way of that helplessness which opens us to the kindness of God. Our very attempt to be godly may lead us to look in the wrong place for God's favor. We may look to our own godliness for the proof of God's favor and fail to see the proof of God's favor where it really is: in the cross of Jesus. That is why Paul reminds us that Christ died for us "while we were yet helpless."

For Paul, therefore, the church is the community of those who are ungodly and know that they are ungodly. The oldest cliché about the church is that it is a community of self-righteous hypocrites. Paul's view of the church is precisely the opposite. For Paul the church is the community of the confessed ungodly. The church is the community of those who do not hypocritically pretend to be better than they are. The church is the community of those who humbly confess precisely who they are and what they are: sinners in the hands of a merciful God. For Paul the church is not the community of the *self*-righteous; for Paul the church is that community which recognizes that righteousness is one thing we cannot give ourselves. Righteousness, a right and whole relationship to one another and to God, is always and only a gift. That gift is given us in the cross of Jesus Christ where God brings us into right relationship with God and with one another.

Just as some of the people to whom Paul wrote were trying to prove their credentials by their godliness, so others were trying to prove their credentials by their status in the world—and particularly by their status as very wise people. Apparently, one of the problems with the church at Corinth at the time that Paul wrote First Corinthians was that there were people there who claimed to be wiser than other people. They assumed that this wisdom gave them some special claim on God's favor. Those of us who live in the academic community and who know how highly wisdom and learning are valued can perhaps best understand the Corinthians if we suggest that they thought that having the right kind of wisdom gave them a kind of cosmic tenure. They could earn God's favor by showing how smart they were. Paul heard that this kind of pride in wisdom was rampant in Corinth, and he wrote a sharp reminder to the Corinthians:

> For consider your call, brethren; not many of you were wise according to worldly standards, not many were powerful, not many were of noble birth; but God chose what is foolish in the world to shame the wise, God chose what is weak in the world to shame the strong, God chose what is low and despised in the world, even things that are not, to bring to nothing things that are, so that no human being might boast in the presence of God (1 Corinthians 1:26-29).

"Boasting" is a bad word for Paul. People who boast are people who still think they live in the Old Age. People who boast are people who don't understand what God has done in Christ Jesus. They are people who think that their importance, their worth, depends on what they have done. Therefore, they boast.

Paul insists that there is only one kind of boasting which is appropriate for Christians; so he reminds the Corinthians at the end of this passage:

[God] is the source of your life in Christ Jesus, whom God made our wisdom, our righteousness and sanctification and redemption; therefore, as it is written, "Let him who boasts, boast of the Lord" (1 Corinthians 1:30-31).

Paul makes it clear that there is only one proper ground for boasting, only one credential in the community without credentials. That ground for boasting, that credential, is the love of God given in Jesus Christ to all people—pious and impious, wise and foolish, of high and low degree.

The Community Without Distinctions

For Paul, if the church is the community without credentials, then it must also be the community without distinctions. When we speak of *credentials,* we speak of our status before God. Those who claim to have credentials claim that they have somehow earned God's favor. Christians know that they haven't earned God's favor and that they needn't earn God's favor, because God's favor is a free gift in the cross of Christ.

When we speak of *distinctions,* we speak of our relationship to other Christians in the church. From the fact that there can be no credentials in the church there follows another fact: there can be no distinctions in the church. Different people may have different skills or different interests, different offices or different responsibilities; but in the crucial matters there are no distinctions. There is nothing which differentiates one Christian from another.

The crucial matters, the matters where there are no distinctions, are two:

(1) ". . . . For there is no distinction; since all have sinned and fall short of the glory of God" (Romans 3:22-23).

(2) ". . . . For there is no distinction; since all . . . are justified by his grace as a gift, through the redemption which is in Christ Jesus" (Romans 3:22-24).

The New Age, the age which began with the cross and resurrection of Jesus Christ, recognizes that these are the only two crucial matters: (1) the fact that everyone sins and (2) the fact that God justifies, makes righteous, loves, redeems, accepts, and helps sinners through Jesus Christ, God's Son.

Although there are all kinds of differences among people in the church (see the next chapter of this book), in the things that count there are no distinctions.

Paul knows that the claim that there are no distinctions in the church has immense practical consequences. Later in Romans he shows how the lack of distinctions between people in the light of the cross has specific implications: "For there is no distinction between Jew and Greek; the same Lord is Lord of all . . ." (Romans 10:12). That is the proof that Christians live in a New Age. In the Old Age nothing was clearer than the distinction between Jews and Greeks. Jews spent lots of time showing how distinct they were from those pagan Greeks; Greeks spent lots of time showing how distinct they were from those superstitious Jews. In the New Age, the age since the cross, there is no distinction. In what counts, Jews and Greeks are one people because they are under one Lord.

Paul makes the implications of this idea even more strikingly clear in the letter to the Galatians. Perhaps he needed to be more striking with the Galatians since they specialized in distinctions— between circumcised males and uncircumcised males, for example. The Galatians claimed that those who acted like Jews were better than those who acted like Greeks. Paul apparently was reminding them of the vows at their baptism, and he says:

> For as many of you as were baptized into Christ have put on Christ. There is neither Jew nor Greek, there is neither slave nor free, there is neither male nor female; for you are all one in Christ Jesus (Galatians 3:27-28).

It is a brand-new world. The old distinctions which seemed so fundamental no longer matter at all. What matters is the fact of God's love in Jesus Christ. That love plays no favorites. Therefore, Christians can play no favorites. The distinction between one race or nation and another, the distinction between one kind of political and economic status and another, even the distinction between being a man and being a woman no longer count.

The old has passed away; the new has come. The church is the community of those who know the new has come. The church is the community which recognizes no distinctions.

The Community Without End

Two of the churches to which Paul wrote had a hard time understanding the relationship of the New Age to the resurrection. The Thessalonians believed what Paul said about the New Age having come. With Paul they also believed that in the New Age God would conquer the forces of sin and death. They believed that in Jesus' resurrection God had already shown God's power to conquer death. They believed that soon Christ would come and complete the

New Age which had begun in his death and resurrection. Now, however, they faced a problem. Some of the members of their church were dying. Did this mean that Christ's resurrection was not effective for them? Did this mean that when the New Age would come in its fullness, those who had died would be cut off from participation in that New Age?

Paul wrote to the Thessalonians in response to their concern for those who had died:

> But we would not have you ignorant, brethren, concerning those who are asleep, that you may not grieve as others do who have no hope. For since we believe that Jesus died and rose again, even so, through Jesus, God will bring with him those who have fallen asleep. For this we declare to you by the word of the Lord, that we who are alive, who are left until the coming of the Lord, shall not precede those who have fallen asleep . . . [all of us] shall always be with the Lord (1 Thessalonians 4:13-17).

The Thessalonians were afraid that death would separate the dead from God's love and from the community of the church. Paul insists that in the community of the New Age those who are dead and those who are alive still belong to one community in the Lord. He insists, therefore, that the fellowship of the New Age is a fellowship without end, since not even death can end that relationship believers have to one another and to Christ.

The Corinthians also had a hard time understanding the relationship of the New Age to the resurrection. Like Paul, they believed in Jesus' resurrection from the dead. Like Paul, they believed that the New Age had already broken in upon human history. However, unlike Paul, they thought that the New Age had already come in its fullness. They thought that there would be no further life beyond this life, no resurrection beyond the grave. They thought there was no need for resurrection since all the goodness of the New Age was right here in this life. Therefore, for the Corinthians, the dead no longer had any part in the New Age because the New Age is an age which consists wholly of life this side of the grave.

Paul wrote to the Corinthians and tried to spell out for them the implications of the faith he had taught them:

> But in fact Christ has been raised from the dead, *the first fruits* of those who have fallen asleep. For as by a man came death, by a man has come also the resurrection of the dead. For as in Adam all die, so also in Christ shall all be made alive (1 Corinthians 15:20-22, author's italics).

Paul here makes two points which are helpful in understanding his belief that the church is a community without end. The first point he makes is that Jesus' resurrection is not an isolated case. Jesus' resurrection is the first fruits of a general resurrection. Jesus' resurrection is the sign that the New Age has begun in earnest. One mark of the New Age is that God conquers death. Since the New Age has begun in earnest, we know that God will conquer death not just for Jesus but for all of us.

The second point Paul makes is a little hard for us to understand. Paul believes that people like you and me take on our character, our attributes from those great figures to whom we belong. Elsewhere Paul talks about believers as children of Abraham because, like Abraham, believers have faith. Christians take on their distinctive features as Christians partly because of their special relationship to Abraham (Galatians 3–4; Romans 4).

Here in 1 Corinthians 15 Paul talks about those characteristics which we have because of our special relationship to Adam and to Christ. We are related to Adam because, like Adam, we all sin "and fall short of the glory of God" (Romans 3:23). We are related to Christ because, in the mercy of God, we are allowed to rise in Christ's resurrection. The *New England Primer* summed up the first of Paul's claims:

> In Adam's fall,
> We sinned all.

Paul's second claim is far more amazing. In Christ's resurrection, we shall all be raised. That means for Paul that the church is not just for the living. Death does not end the relationship of faithful people to the risen Lord. Just as he was raised, so they will be raised. More than that, they will be raised "in him." That means they will be raised in continued fellowship with him and with one another.

There is a traditional phrase for Paul's belief that the church is a community without end. That phrase is the "communion of saints." It suggests that the Thessalonians were wrong to worry about the Christians who had died, as if they were cut off from full and lasting fellowship with Christ. It suggests that the Corinthians were wrong to ignore the Christians who had died, as if their relationship to Christ and to other Christians no longer mattered. The belief in the "communion of saints" suggests that Christians, both living and dead, are united to Christ and to one another for all eternity. The church is not just that bunch of people who happen to be alive and on the church rolls at this very minute. The church extends back to the very earliest Christians and includes the faithful of all ages and will include us—even after we have died.

Paul sums up that faith in the communion of saints, the community without end, in one of his great affirmations:

> None of us lives to himself, and none of us dies to himself. If we live, we live to the Lord, and if we die, we die to the Lord; so then, whether we live or whether we die, we are the Lord's (Romans 14:7-8).

The Reluctant Community

Paul is not talking about the ideal church. He is talking about the real church. He is not talking about the way the church is supposed to be; he is talking about the way the church really is. For Paul there really *is* a new creation in Jesus Christ. The church really is the community which shares in that new creation. The real church is the church without credentials, without distinctions, and without end.

There was, however, a problem. Those specific churches to which Paul wrote sometimes didn't act like the real church. They sometimes acted as if they still lived entirely in the Old Age. They sometimes seemed to forget that the New Age had broken into history in the cross and resurrection of Jesus Christ. They sometimes forgot that they were supposed to live as citizens of that New Age which was already impinging on the world and would one day reach its glorious consummation.

The problem, therefore, was that the churches sometimes forgot to be what they were—the communities of the New Age. The problem was that they acted out of a false understanding of themselves, as if they still lived in the Old Age. Paul was constantly reminding the churches to be what they were:

> If anyone is in Christ, there is a new creation; the old has passed away, behold, the new has come. All this is from God, who through Christ reconciled us to himself and gave us the ministry of reconciliation; that is, God was in Christ, reconciling the world to himself. . . . We beseech you on behalf of Christ, *be reconciled to God* (2 Corinthians 5:17-20, with author's italics and emendations).

There is the characteristic Pauline exhortation: you do live in a new creation; now act like it. You *are* reconciled to God; therefore, *be* reconciled to God. Be who you are.

The churches really were communities without credentials, but Paul had to remind the Galatians that it didn't matter whether they were circumcised and kept the Jewish law or not (Galatians 3). He had to remind the Corinthians that it didn't matter whether they were especially wise or not (1 Corinthians 1). Paul wrote to remind his churches to be what they were: communities in which neither godliness nor wisdom count for anything; only God's love in Jesus Christ counts.

The churches really were communities without distinctions, but Paul had to remind the Romans that there was no special privilege in being either a Jew or a Greek (Romans 10:12). He had to remind the Corinthians that there were many gifts from God and that no gift gave them the right to act as if they were more important than their brothers or sisters (1 Corinthians 12). He had to remind both the Romans and the Corinthians that those who have strong faith and therefore do not worry about obeying the details of the law should not offend those who are weaker in faith (Romans 14; 1 Corinthians 8). In almost every one of Paul's letters we see the signs that there were fights and feuds and dissension in the churches to which he wrote. Constantly he had to remind them to be what they were: the community without distinctions, the one body of Christ.

The churches were communities without end. Yet, as we have seen, Paul had to assure the Thessalonians and the Corinthians that they would not be forever separated from their dead (1 Thessalonians 4; 1 Corinthians 15). Both the Thessalonians and the Corinthians neglected to be what they were: the communion of saints. Both feared or pretended that their union with Christ was possible in this life only. Paul wrote to remind them of what they were—the church without end, the church where the living and the dead live and die in the Lord.

Paul never gave up on the church, not even on any one church. Even in the case of the Galatians, where he was disappointed and angry, he cared and hoped enough to write them his disappointment and his anger. He believed that the most important fact about the churches was that they were communities "in Christ." (See Romans 1:6; 1 Corinthians 1:2; Philippians 1:1; 1 Thessalonians 1:1; and even Galatians 6:18.) In Christ, there is a new creation, a New Age. The churches, therefore, really were the communities of that New Age, even when they tried to pretend that they lived in the old world of credentials, distinctions, and death.

The Community Today

In some ways Paul's concerns seem foreign and old-fashioned to us. We are not much worried about circumcision or keeping the

Jewish law. Our disputes are probably not over official "teachers of wisdom" in our churches. If we are concerned about the resurrection of the dead, we don't put that concern in the same terms that the Thessalonians or the Corinthians did.

Yet in the issues which really matter, there is no distinction, as Paul would say, between his churches and our own. We, too, are asked to live as communities of the New Age; and we, too, tend to behave as if we still lived in the Old Age.

Like Paul's churches we are really communities without credentials. We don't act as if we were communities without credentials, but we really are. We sometimes act as if what makes the church so special is that we are especially godly people—especially pious, especially religious, or especially ethical. We know that that isn't so. We know that we are who we are only because God in Christ has loved us as we are—impious, irreligious, and not especially ethical.

We sometimes act as if the church were especially wise. We act as if we've figured out a whole series of crucial facts which the poor, stupid people outside the church haven't discovered. Secretly we know that we're the church because God has chosen to do the most foolish thing of all—to love all God's children, in Jesus Christ. That's the one fact we've figured out; and if we've figured it out, it's not because we're so bright. It's because God stuck that fact right out in front of our noses until it was absolutely impossible for us to ignore it any longer.

The church is the community without credentials. It is the community which recognizes only one set of credentials—the credentials of the crucified One. The church is the community which dares not boast or, if it boasts, can boast only in its Lord.

Like the church in Paul's time we are really communities without distinctions. We don't act as if we were communities without distinctions, but we really are.

We sometimes act as if one could transplant all the distinctions from the Old Age into the New Age and they would fit just beautifully. We sometimes act as if we could use the old distinctions between professionals and lay people, not as a way of dividing responsibilities, but as a way of distinguishing worthiness. We sometimes pretend that only clergy can provide spiritual truth or loving-kindness or can give invocations at church dinners. We know that that isn't so, but we sometimes pretend it is.

Or we pretend that it's crucially important whether we are theological "evangelicals" or "liberals." We split churches. We set up competing seminaries. We pretend that evangelicals and liberals are not equally marked by sin and delivered by the grace of God in the cross of Christ. We know that that distinction doesn't hold for the New Age, but we keep pretending that it does.

Or we pretend that the marks of status which count in the rest of society should count in the church. The same people who are highly honored in our towns should be highly honored in the churches. People with prestigious professions should have prestigious offices. Full professors should have more power than assistant professors and certainly more power than students. We pretend that the distinctions of the world make a difference in the church as well. We know that that isn't so, but we pretend it is.

Or we pretend that it makes a difference whether one is male or female in the church in the New Age. We know perfectly well what Paul said: "[In Christ]. . . there is neither male nor female" (Galatians 3:28); but we pretend that we don't understand. We have one board of deacons to do the spiritual work and one board of deaconesses to do the dirty work. We want only ushers who wear suits, and pantsuits won't do. We have heard rumors that more and more women are graduating from our seminaries and that some of them are highly competent. We wish them well, but we don't want to hire them as OUR ministers. We know, of course, that that is sheer fakery. We know that the distinction between male and female belongs to a different world, a different age, from the church. We know that the distinctions cannot hold, but we keep pretending that they can.

Or we pretend that race makes a difference in the church. We pretend *that* with a vengeance. We pretend it frantically every Sunday morning when, for the most part, whites pretend they are supposed to worship with whites, Latinos with Latinos, blacks with blacks, Asian-Americans with Asian-Americans, and Native Americans with Native Americans. We know that that worship is unfaithful. We know that that worship is a false picture of the true church, where there is neither Jew, nor Greek, nor white, Latino, black, Asian-American, nor Native American. We give reasons for our divisions. We speak of worship styles and ethnic pride, but we know that those excuses will not do for long. We know perfectly well who we really are: we are the one people of the one Lord, without distinctions, without divisions, without nations, and without race. We long and pray and work for the day when we will be who we really are.

Finally, like the church in Paul's time we are really the church without end. We are really the communion of saints. We sometimes pretend that we're not the communion of saints, but we are.

We pretend that we can skip directly from the New Testament to the twentieth century and pay no attention to our fathers and mothers in the faith. We pretend that the church cares only about Jesus and today's newspaper, and we neglect Ignatius and Augustine and Saint Theresa and Calvin and Martin Luther and Martin Luther King. We know that Ignatius and Augustine and Theresa and Calvin and Luther and King are part of one community with us, but we pretend that that isn't so.

We pretend that we can simply reinvent theology and worship and teaching in each generation. We pretend that what the church has done in other ages and other places makes no difference for us. We know that we are really one church—through all ages and in all places—but we pretend that that isn't so.

Or we turn it around. We assume that the only church is the church of our fathers and mothers. We pretend that we can simply pick up their faith and swallow it whole. We pretend that we can simply repeat their words and reenact their liturgies. We pretend that they are not joined with us in a living church, a church which grows and changes in the freedom of the living Lord.

We know, of course, exactly who we are. We know that we are part of the communion of saints. We know that we are joined to the Christian faithful of all ages, learning from them, honoring them. We know that the Christian faithful of all ages are joined to us, that they have prepared the way for us and for the new concerns and faithfulness which we must bring. We know more than that; we know that we are preparing the way for Christians to come. We know that we are called to transmit to them the faith we have received in the terms which we best understand. We know that we are called to affirm their freedom to accept that faith in the terms they best understand.

Sometimes we pretend that the church is just us, right now, without ancestors and without offspring in the faith. But we know it isn't so. We know that we and our ancestors and our children are part of the communion of saints, the community of faith without end.

We know who we really are. We are the community of the New Age, a community without credentials, without distinctions, without end. We pray to God that we may *be* who we really are: the church of Jesus Christ our Lord, in whom the old has passed away and the new has come.

Questions for Discussion

1. Why does Paul believe that the whole world has changed— that "there is a new creation" for the believer?

2. What are the ways in which we sometimes try to prove our "credentials"? How can our church live more fully as a community which does not stress credentials?

3. How can the structures and programs of our church better represent Paul's insistence that the church is a community which doesn't recognize distinctions among people?

4. What implications does the Christian belief in the "communion of saints" have for the teaching ministry of our church?

5. Paul believes that God's love is a sheer gift, given in the cross of Jesus Christ. If we believe that, what difference does it make in the life of our own congregation?

2

How Does the *Whole* Church Teach?

For us, as for Paul, the church is the community of the New Age. The fact that we are the community of the New Age has crucial implications for our ministry. It means, for one thing, that we are called to recruit citizens for the New Age. This ministry is usually called evangelism. It means, for another thing, that we have the responsibility for training people to be good and faithful citizens of the New Age. We have the responsibility for instructing people in the civics of the kingdom. This ministry is usually called teaching However, for Paul the distinction between evangelism and teaching is not nearly as clear as we try to make it. When Paul preaches the gospel, when he evangelizes, he includes in his preaching the concern for the responsibilities and obligations of citizenship in the church and the kingdom. When Paul "teaches" the fundamentals of good citizenship, he regularly recalls his readers to the word of the gospel with which their faith began. For Paul, as for us, both evangelism and instruction can be seen as part of the teaching ministry of the church.

Since the church for Paul is a community without distinctions, we can assume that this fundamental teaching ministry of the church is not just entrusted to some Christians and denied to others. Since we are really joined in *one* community, all of us are involved in the church's task of teaching. All of us are involved in the two responsibilities of evangelism and education.

In the twelfth chapter of First Corinthians Paul writes at length about the ministry of the whole church. In the following pages we shall look carefully at 1 Corinthians 12 to see what clues it provides for understanding our teaching ministry. We shall examine the two main themes of that chapter:

(1) For Paul the church is a community which has *variety* but no distinctions.

(2) For Paul the church is the community which is the body of Christ.

The Community with Variety but No Distinctions

We have already seen that Paul believes that the church is a community without distinctions. That is, he believes that no church member is more important or more valuable than any other church member. Church members are not to vaunt themselves over one another or to bicker with one another on the basis of national background, race, social status, or any of those other "distinctions" which seemed so important in the Old Age.

The Corinthian church, however, despite Paul's admonitions, seems to have specialized in distinctions. As we noted, for the Corinthians the most important distinction was the distinction based on wisdom. The Corinthians argued with one another over who was the wisest among them. Apparently, those who claimed to be especially wise thought that they should have more prestige and more authority in the church than their less brilliant brothers and sisters.

There was another element to this stress on the distinctive value of wisdom. Apparently, the Corinthians were arguing about the wisdom of their church leaders and especially about the wisdom of the various early apostles. Some Corinthians had attached themselves to one apostle, claiming that he was especially wise. Other Corinthians had attached themselves to another apostle and claimed that, compared to this apostle, their opponents' favorite was a very dull fellow indeed. One group apparently even thought that they had a special claim on Christ, as if he were just the wisest of early Christian leaders and not God's Promised One for *all* people— without distinction.

When Paul heard of the emphasis on different leaders and their special wisdom, he was not pleased (even though he was one of the apostles cited as especially wise). He wrote to the Corinthians:

> I appeal to you, brethren, by the name of our Lord Jesus Christ, that all of you agree and that there be no dissensions among you, but that you be united in the same mind and the same judgment. For it has been reported to me by Chloe's people that there is quarreling among you, my brethren. What I mean is that each one of you says, "I belong to Paul," or "I belong to Apollos," or "I belong to Cephas [Peter]," or "I belong to Christ." Is Christ divided? . . . (1 Corinthians 1:10-13).

There is another kind of distinction in which the Corinthian church specialized: the distinction between the rich and the poor. This showed itself in a particularly nasty way. When the Corinthians came together to observe the Lord's Supper, the rich brought baskets full of food and drink. Then they stuffed themselves and got drunk. Not only was this intemperate, but it was also unkind. Those Christians who could afford little were forced to sit and watch their wealthy brothers and sisters make pigs and fools of themselves, and this at the table of the Lord! Paul was appalled:

> When you meet together, it is not the Lord's supper that you eat. For in eating, each one goes ahead with his own meal, and one is hungry, and another is drunk. What! Do you not have houses to eat and drink in? Or do you despise the church of God and humiliate those who have nothing? What shall I say to you? Shall I commend you in this? No, I will not (1 Corinthians 11:20-22).

The Corinthians were concerned with yet a third kind of distinction. They were concerned with the distinction between those who had some special skill and those who didn't. This concern with distinctions evidently lay behind the twelfth chapter of First Corinthians. Apparently, some Corinthians were bragging because they were good teachers while others weren't. Some Corinthians were bragging because they were good preachers while others weren't. And some Corinthians were bragging because they could speak in tongues while others couldn't. Indeed, this stress on the "distinction" of being able to speak in tongues seems to have been the most distressing element of the Corinthians' boasting divisiveness. Of course, while those who could teach well or preach well or speak in tongues were loudly flaunting their special accomplishments, those who could not teach well or preach well or speak in tongues were feeling left out and sorry for themselves.

When Paul heard of the proud and unloving stress on distinctions in Corinth, he made a helpful observation. He observed that it is fine and necessary for the church to have *variety* but that it is wrong and harmful for the church to have distinctions.

Paul acknowledged the need for variety in part because he had eyes to see, and he knew that variety is an undeniable part of the church's life. He had to listen to preaching, and he knew that not everyone is a good preacher. (Indeed, he sometimes suggested that he was not a very good preacher, though that hardly kept him from preaching; cf. 1 Corinthians 2:1-5; 2 Corinthians 11:6.) He had sat through worship services, and he knew that some people could speak in tongues and others couldn't. (He could, incidentally, though he didn't make much of it; see 1 Corinthians 14:18-19.)

However, all this variety, which Paul can't deny and doesn't want to deny, has nothing to do with *distinctions*. The fact that some people have one talent, some another, doesn't make some people better than others; it just makes them different.

For Paul there are two reasons why the fact of variety in the church cannot indicate that there are distinctions in the church.

The first reason is that Paul has always argued that there are NO distinctions regarding the two great facts: (1) that all have sinned and (2) that all are saved by grace. (Cf. Romans 3:21-25.) And obviously *these* are the important facts about us. The facts of our sin and God's grace are so important that we can't even talk about those great facts and the little variety of our talents in the same breath. We can't say, "I'm a sinner saved by grace, and I'm a good preacher" in the same breath without sounding ridiculous. The first part of that sentence is infinitely more significant than the second part. It's as if someone said, "I've just fallen in love with Marjorie, and I got this tie for only three dollars." We sound silly when we mix up great facts with trivial facts. When we have really acknowledged the great facts—that we are sinners saved by grace—we barely have breath left to boast of the little facts—that we preach or teach well or speak in tongues.

The second reason that Paul accepts variety in the church but rejects distinctions in the church is that Paul has an overwhelming commitment to the unity of the church. Nothing is more important to Paul than the conviction that the church is *one*. Whenever people start boasting of their distinctions, they start breaking up into little cliques. The supposedly wise people separate themselves from the supposedly not-so-wise. Paul's devotees separate themselves from Peter's devotees. Good speakers form a little public speakers club and exclude poor speakers from membership. Those who speak in tongues form the Fellowship of Corinthian Charismatics and inform noncharismatics that they are not worthy to join. This kind of divisiveness annoys Paul beyond measure. Variety is all right (indeed, variety is a gift of God), but distinctions are all wrong. They are all wrong because they bring division within one church.

When Paul speaks about variety within the church, what does he mean? How does he think it possible for the church to have variety and unity at the same time? Paul makes his argument in 1 Corinthians 12:4-5:

> Now there are varieties of gifts, but the same Spirit; and there are varieties of service, but the same Lord.

Each of these phrases is worth careful study.

(1) "There are varieties of gifts, but the same Spirit."

Paul readily admits that there is variety in the church. Some are good preachers; some are good teachers; some do speak with tongues. But the variety is a variety of _gifts_.

When Paul writes of gifts, he means gifts from God. One reason that variety is a good thing is that variety comes from God. In this sense the church is like creation itself. Just as God has shown forth the diversity of God's bounty in the gifts of creation, so God has shown forth the diversity of God's bounty in the gifts of the church. The fact that gifts come from God makes them radically different from distinctions, which come from people. It is people who give out ribbons and medals and hoods and letters to put after our names— like B.A., M.D., or Ph.D. It is God who gives various talents and skills.

Furthermore, if the variety in the church is really a variety of gifts, that means that the Corinthians (and we) can't take credit for that variety. The variety isn't a matter of what we have earned or accomplished; the variety is a matter of what we have been _given_. Only very small children at Christmastime think that what they have been given is anything to brag about. Mature people know that gifts can only be received, quietly, gratefully. So when the Corinthians wanted to brag about how wise they were or how eloquent they were, Paul replied: "You didn't accomplish your wisdom or eloquence. You didn't earn your wisdom or eloquence. Your wisdom and eloquence are gifts." When the Corinthians wanted to brag about speaking in tongues, Paul said: "Speaking in tongues is a gift; and since it's a gift, what is there to brag about? What is there to hit another Christian over the head with? If it's a gift, it's a gift. Be grateful, and then be still."

Paul makes the point wonderfully clear in 1 Corinthians 4:7: ". . . . What have you that you did not receive? If then you received it, why do you boast as if it were not a gift?" (Perhaps we should frame that verse and hang it in every church office, every seminary classroom, every graduate school cubicle, and certainly every faculty office—even at the University of Chicago.)

The variety to which Paul points is a variety of gifts. The unity to which he points is the unity of the Spirit. "There are varieties of gifts, but the same Spirit."

For Paul the Spirit is the great sign of citizenship in the New Age. The mark of being in the New Age is precisely that you have received the gift of God's presence—God's Spirit.

"And because you are [God's] sons, God has sent the Spirit of his Son into our hearts, crying, 'Abba! Father!' So through God you are no longer a slave but a son, and if a son then an heir" (Galatians 4:6-7).

"So then, brethren, we are debtors, not to the flesh, to live according to the flesh—for if you live according to the flesh you will die, but if by the Spirit you put to death the deeds of the body you will live. For all who are led by the Spirit of God are sons of God" (Romans 8:12-14).

However, for Paul the presence of the Spirit cannot be identified with any *one* gift of the Spirit. The same Spirit is manifest in a diversity of gifts. So the good preacher can't say to another Christian, "If you don't preach well, you haven't received the Spirit; you are not a citizen of the New Age." The charismatic Corinthian can't say to the Corinthian Christian who doesn't speak in tongues, "Since you don't speak in tongues, you haven't received the Spirit. You don't live in the New Age." Preaching, speaking in tongues, teaching, and prophesying are all gifts of the Spirit; but no one of those gifts is *required* as proof of the Spirit's presence.

Indeed, Paul goes on to write: "To each is given the manifestation of the Spirit for the *common good*" (1 Corinthians 12:7, author's italics). Since the gifts of the Spirit are given for the common good, we can be sure that any boasting of one particular gift of the Spirit at the expense of others is a misuse of the Spirit. We can be sure that any flaunting of the gifts of the Spirit to bring divisiveness rather than unity in the church is a misuse of the Spirit.

There are three gifts of the Spirit which every Christian receives. Every Christian receives these precisely because they are essential to the *unity* of the church. These gifts are faith, hope, and love (1 Corinthians 13:13). These gifts are the true marks of the Spirit's presence. They are the necessary signs of life in the New Age.

Paul claims that where faith, hope, and love are, the Spirit of God is present whether or not there is preaching, prophesying, speaking in tongues, or healing. Where faith, hope, and especially love are not, the Spirit of God is not present, even though the preaching be eloquent, the prophesying astonishingly accurate, the speaking in tongues ecstatic, and the healing miracles beyond number. We can put this another way: where a church is growing in faith, in hope, and especially in love, the Spirit of God is there. Where a church is bickering over faith, slack in hope, and forgetful of love, it serves a fake and foreign spirit—under whatever pious name that spirit may go.

(2) "There are varieties of service, but the same Lord."

Again, Paul sets the church's variety in a proper perspective. The variety is a variety of *service*.

The word Paul uses here literally means "table service" (and it is the root word for our word "deacon"). His use of the word should have had a humbling effect on the boastful Corinthians. All this diversity they bragged of was really just a diversity of table service. When God gave some of them the ability to preach, some the ability to teach, some the ability to prophesy, and others the ability to speak in tongues, it was as if God had said, "All right, some of you are to carry in the silverware; some of you are to fill the plates; some of you do the dishes, and some of you sweep up after dinner." That is a very modest view of the various functions people serve in the church.

The word "service" also reminded the Corinthians of the purpose for which they had received this variety of gifts. They had been given these gifts, not in order to brag about their distinctive talents, but in order to be of service—each in his or her own special way. The Corinthians were not supposed to say: "This is my particular talent, my special skill." They were supposed to say: "This is my kind of service; this is the way in which I can help." When Paul spoke of their service, he turned the Corinthians immediately from themselves to others. He turned them from asking what they deserved from others to asking what they could do for others.

Once more Paul moves from the proper understanding of the

church's variety to the proper stress on the church's unity: "There is the same Lord."

Again, this puts the life of the Christian in an appropriately humbling perspective. The tendency for the Corinthians had been to lord it over one another, precisely on the basis of the variety of service which the Corinthians had received. Paul reminded the Corinthians that they couldn't lord it over one another because they were all *under* one Lord—namely, Jesus Christ.

His phrase here picks up the image of the table service. Those who serve the table have nothing to brag of in their service—their sweeping, setting the silver, or washing the plates. What they do have to brag of is the Lord of the table, the Host whom they serve. The picture recalls Paul's earlier words to the Corinthians:

> God chose what is low and despised in the world, even things that are not, to bring to nothing things that are, so that no human being might boast in the presence of God . . . therefore, as it is written, "Let him who boasts, boast of the Lord" (1 Corinthians 1:28-31).

The reminder of Christ's lordship is also the reminder of the inescapable basis of our unity. It is the lordship of Christ which brought the Corinthians together as one church, even in their variety. It is fine that some of the Corinthians spoke well, some sang well, some spoke impressively in tongues. It is far finer and far more crucial that all the Corinthians served one Lord. When they came together, the Corinthians should not have come together to compare gifts or flaunt their achievements. They should have come together to praise and acknowledge the one Lord, who was the source of their life and of their salvation.

Therefore, according to Paul, variety is a good and necessary part of the church's life as long as we recognize it for what it is. Variety is not a variety of attainments but a variety of gifts. Variety is not a variety of what the world owes us but a variety of what we owe the world in loving service. That is, variety is a good and necessary part of our lives, but we dare not confuse variety with distinctions. We need to remember that our variety does not provide ground for boasting or for divisiveness. We need to remember that in the things which matter there are no distinctions. We have all received one Spirit. We all serve one Lord.

The Church as the Body of Christ

After writing about the variety and unity of the church, Paul

goes on to draw his great picture of the community of the New Age—
the picture of the church as the body of Christ. Here and in Romans
12:3ff. Paul makes explicit an assumption which lies behind much of
his understanding of the church. In part he uses the familiar picture of
a social group as a body to stress the interdependent nature of the
church.[1] In part, it is the church's unique role as the body of *Christ*
which informs Paul's understanding of the church both in these
passages and elsewhere in his writings.

The Church as a Body

The image of the church as a body allows Paul to make several
telling arguments against the Corinthians' stress on the importance of
distinctions within the church.

First, Paul uses the image of the body to show that variety in the
church is part of the church's strength, not part of its weakness. Those
who believe in distinctions seem to think that everyone should want
the same gifts. Good preachers think everyone should want to be a
good preacher. Those who perform healings think everyone should
want to do the same. Those who speak in tongues think everyone
should earnestly desire the gift of glossolalia. The picture of the
church as a body indicates that a variety of gifts is part of the church's
strength:

> The body does not consist of one member but of many. If the foot should
> say, "Because I am not a hand, I do not belong to the body," that would not
> make it any less a part of the body. And if the ear should say, "Because I am
> not an eye, I do not belong to the body," that would not make it any less a
> part of the body. If the whole body were an eye, where would be the
> hearing? If the whole body were an ear, where would be the sense of smell?
> But as it is, God arranged the organs in the body, each one of them, as he
> chose. . . . As it is, there are many parts, yet one body. The eye cannot say to
> the hand, "I have no need of you," nor again the head to the feet, "I have no
> need of you" (1 Corinthians 12:14-21).

There are three clear implications of Paul's insistence that the
church's variety is part of its strength.

For one thing, Paul again reminds the Corinthians that the
variety in their life is a gift from God. *"God* arranged the organs in the
body, each one of them, as he chose." They are not to seek uniformity
within the church or be ashamed of diversity. That diversity is a gift
of God.

For another thing, Paul reminds the Corinthians that no one is
to be ashamed of the gifts which he or she has received (or hasn't

received). The Corinthians are not to say, "Because I am not a hand, I do not belong to the body." That is, those who are not preachers should not feel any less a part of the church than those who are. Those who are not teachers are no less a part of the church than those who teach. Those who do not speak in tongues are no less a part of the church than those who do.

And then further, Paul reminds the Corinthians that no member of the church can glory in self-sufficient pride. A variety of gifts is necessary for the life of every member of the church. "The eye cannot say to the hand, 'I have no need of you.'" Paul's point here is not just that the eye and the hand are equally important and valuable— though that is part of what he means. More than that, Paul's point is that the eye and the hand need each other. They are interdependent parts of the body. Applied to the Corinthian situation, this suggests that those who can preach need those who can teach; those who speak in tongues need those who can prophesy; the choir needs the sexton, and the Corinthian Board of Deacons needs the Corinthian Women's Missionary Society. None can say to the others: "I have no need of you."

Not only does Paul use the picture of the church as a body to insist that variety is part of the church's strength, but he also uses the picture of the church as a body to show what kind of a community the church is. The church is a community of *sympathy*.

The word "sympathy" means "feeling with" someone else. Paul insists that the church is the community of people who feel with one another. We feel with one another not because that's a nice Christian thing to do but because we have no choice. We feel with one another because we are interdependent. We feel with one another because we are part of one body. In our own lives, if we stub a toe, our whole body hurts. If we eat a good meal, our whole body rejoices— assuming that we don't overeat. So it is with the church. When the church's toe is stubbed, the whole church hurts. When the church's stomach is full, the whole church rejoices. When someone in the church at Corinth loses a loved one, all suffer that loss. It doesn't matter whether the bereaved is a member of the same club or board or sings in the choir or not. All mourn. When someone in the church at Corinth receives an honor, all rejoice, whether or not the person honored is a member of their own special circle of friends. Most important, Corinthians will certainly not feel jealousy or rancor when someone else gets an honor which they themselves lack. So Paul writes: "[Let] there . . . be no discord in the body, . . . that the members may have the same care for one another. If one member suffers, all suffer together; if one member is honored, all rejoice together" (1 Corinthians 12:25-26).

This image of the church as a body underlines the description of the church as a new community which we have stressed in this book.

Since the church is one body, it is a community without credentials. Paul writes: "God has so composed the body, giving the greater honor to the inferior part" (1 Corinthians 12:24). That is, in the eyes of God there is a kind of balance of honor within the church. In the economy of grace no person is relegated to inferior status. There is no place in the body of Christ either for boasting or for shame, because the body of Christ is that community in which credentials do not count.

Since the church is one body, it is a community without distinctions. No Christian can turn boastfully to his or her neighbor, saying: "I am more important than you are. I am more useful than you are." That kind of boastful stress on distinctions negates the essential unity of the body, where there should be "no discord . . . but . . . the members [should] have the same care for one another" (1 Corinthians 12:25).

Since the church is one body, it is a community without end. In this respect, 1 Corinthians 12 must be seen in the light of 1 Corinthians 15. Just as Christ's body was raised a spiritual body for all eternity, so Christians are part of his body for all eternity. Death can bring to Christians no lasting separation from Christ or from each other.[2]

The Church as the Body of Christ

Though Paul has probably taken over the image of the church as a body from some of the common metaphors of his time, when he refers to the church as the body of Christ, he is not speaking metaphorically but realistically.[3] This realism permeates Paul's entire understanding of the church. When Paul claims that in baptism we die and rise with Christ, he doesn't mean that it is *as if* we died and rose with Christ. He means that as Christ was crucified by the powers of the Old Age, we, too, die to the Old Age in baptism. As Christ was raised by the power of God as the first fruits of the New Age, so we are raised by the power of God out of the baptismal waters into citizenship in that New Age:

> Do you not know that all of us who have been baptized into Christ Jesus were baptized into his death? We were buried therefore with him by baptism into death, so that as Christ was raised from the dead by the glory of the Father, we too might walk in newness of life (Romans 6:3-4).

When Paul writes about the Lord's Supper, he doesn't mean that when we take the bread and the cup it is *as if* we were sharing in Christ's body and blood. He means we *do* share in Christ's body and blood. (He, of course, makes no claims about the hows or the wherefores; that was for later church debate.)

> The cup of blessing which we bless, is it not a participation [or fellowship] in the blood of Christ? The bread which we break, is it not a participation [or fellowship] in the body of Christ? Because there is one bread, we who are many are one body, for we all partake of the one bread (1 Corinthians 10:16-17).

So, too, when Paul writes about the church as the body of Christ, he doesn't simply say that we should conduct ourselves *as if* we were the body of Christ. He says that the church *is* Christ's body.

> Now you are the body of Christ and individually members of it (1 Corinthians 12:27).

> We, though many, are one body in Christ, and individually members one of another (Romans 12:5).

For Paul, just as Christ's spiritual body is now exalted with God the Father, so Christ's physical, earthly body is present and active in Corinth, Rome, Thessalonica, and Philippi.

This has a crucial implication for our understanding of the church. Since the church really is the body of Christ, we need to understand the church not just as a "body" but as the body of the crucified and risen Lord whom we serve.

For Paul *the church is the body of the crucified Lord.* In Romans 7:4*a* Paul writes: "Likewise, my brethren, you have died to the law through the body of Christ," implying that membership in the body of Christ implies a real death to the Old Age. So, too, the passages on the Lord's Supper in 1 Corinthians 10:16 and 11:23-27 make clear that for Paul membership in the body of Christ is, in part, membership in the broken body of the crucified One.

We know enough about Paul's understanding of the cross of Christ to know what it might mean for the church to be the body of the crucified One.

The church which is the body of the crucified One is a church which is open to the possibility of brokenness. It is a church which does not always glory in its strength but sometimes rejoices in its weakness. It is a church which does not measure its faithfulness by how successful it is in terms of the world's standards. It is a church which may have to measure its faithfulness by how broken it is for the sake of the world's needs. It is a church which is willing to be weak when compassion requires weakness. It is a church whose members are willing even to be weak for the sake of each other. It is a church whose members are willing to admit and share their vulnerability. It is a church whose members are willing to accept and affirm the vulnerabilities of one another.

The church which is the body of the crucified One is a church which is open to the possibility of disgrace. Paul thinks that the Corinthians are so concerned about trying to show that they are as wise and prestigious as those outside the church that they forget the scandal, the disgrace of the cross. Today we have a hard time recapturing the sheer offensiveness of the cross. In our time the cross is so often a little gold trinket worn on a chain or a neon sign on the side of the church that we forget its original power as the symbol of ultimate outrage and disgrace. Probably we would get a better sense of the disgrace if we walked into our churches some Sunday morning to find an electric chair before the altar, or at least a stark wooden cross large enough to hold a man, with a nail or two to remind us of the pain. The church's Lord was crucified as an outlaw, as one who stood outside all the canons of law, decency, and good taste.

The church which is the body of the disgraced One is not concerned—as the Corinthians were concerned—with being socially acceptable or prestigious in its community. It is a church which is not concerned that its building or the appointments thereof should meet the high economic standards of the surrounding community. It is a church which is not concerned that its every pronouncement be acceptable to the prevailing intellectual prejudices of the nearby academy (though the scandal of the cross should not be confused with the scandal of inarticulate or self-contradictory theology). It is a church which does not take a Gallup poll to determine the prevailing ethical winds in its community before taking its stand on compelling social issues. The church which is the body of the disgraced and crucified One may stand disgracefully apart from the economic and aesthetic standards of its community. It may proclaim the intellectually scandalous word that the love of God has been acted out for all humankind in a place of public execution. It may stand foolishly against the deeply cherished ethical principles of its neighbors.

The church which is the body of the crucified One is a church which is open to the possibility of risk. It knows that the crucified One was and is no cautious Lord. The church takes risks as an institution, knowing that what it loses will ultimately count for more than what it preserves. It encourages personal risks among its members—the risk of caring and, harder yet, the risk of admitting that we need care: "If one member suffers, all suffer together; if one member is honored, all rejoice together" (1 Corinthians 12:26).

For Paul *the church is the body of the risen Lord.* This, I think, is the theological presupposition behind 1 Corinthians 12 and Romans 12. For Paul the risen Lord has not simply gone to be with God the Father on a heavenly throne. The risen Lord is alive and well and active in the lives of specific congregations.

The church which is the body of the risen Lord is a church which acknowledges Christ's presence. Paul writes of the Lord's Supper: "Any one who eats and drinks without discerning the body eats and drinks judgment upon himself" (1 Corinthians 11:29). Here Paul acknowledges that Christ is genuinely present in the worship of the community. Paul's frequent reference to Christians as those "in Christ" also affirms that the church serves no distant Lord but one who is present and active in the church's life.

The church as the body of the risen Lord is a church which acknowledges Christ's power. For Paul the church is not just a community where people learn things. It is a community where lives are changed. He speaks of the power of the living Lord most directly in connection with the church's preaching ministry:

> For Jews demand signs and Greeks seek wisdom, but we preach Christ crucified, a stumbling block to Jews and folly to Gentiles, but to those who are called, both Jews and Greeks, Christ the power of God and the wisdom of God (1 Corinthians 1:22-24).

That is, for Paul the crucified One is also the risen One, who is present in power in the witnessing life of the church. In another puzzling passage in First Corinthians, Paul is instructing the Corinthians on how to excommunicate a man who has behaved shamefully. He says, ". . . . When you are assembled, and my spirit is present, with the power of our Lord Jesus, you are to deliver this man to Satan for the destruction of the flesh, that his spirit may be saved in the day of the

Lord Jesus" (1 Corinthians 5:4-5). This is a very difficult passage, but at least it indicates Paul's faith that the power of the risen Lord is a real and active force in the life of the church. The church which is the body of the risen Lord acknowledges and relies on the power of the Christ who is present in its midst.

For Paul the church as the body of the risen Lord is also a church which acknowledges Christ's *ongoing* authority as teacher. In common with much of the early church, Paul believes that Christ's teaching ministry did not end with the crucifixion and resurrection. For Paul the teachings of the earthly Jesus still have authoritative force because that Jesus has been acknowledged as Lord by the resurrection from the dead. For example, in 1 Corinthians 7:10-11 Paul uses a teaching of the earthly Jesus (cf. Mark 10:2-12) and insists that it carries the authority of the living Lord: "To the married I give charge, not I but the Lord, that the wife should not separate from her husband . . . and that the husband should not divorce his wife." More than that, the living Lord apparently continues to instruct the church through authoritative teachers and prophets. *New* teachings are also attributed to the risen Lord. For example, in 1 Corinthians 14, Paul is writing the Corinthian church about the role of prophets. He claims that his instructions carry Christ's own authority, although we have no record of any saying of the earthly Jesus pertaining to this issue, and it is unlikely that the earthly Jesus would have been concerned with this later problem of order in the church community. Paul writes: "If any one thinks that he is a prophet, or spiritual, he should acknowledge that what I am writing to you is a command of the Lord" (1 Corinthians 14:37). The context also suggests that the validity of this word of the Lord is not to be tested by referring to memories of the earthly Jesus but by a spiritual test of the instructions' present authenticity. All of this points to a very complicated issue in our understanding of the life of the early church; but the heart of my claim is that Paul believes that Jesus, the risen Lord, continues to exercise teaching authority in the church even after his death and resurrection. For Paul an appeal to the word of the Lord is not always an appeal to the words Jesus pronounced during his ministry; sometimes it is an appeal to the Lord who is still present in the church's teaching ministry.

We can summarize the suggestions of this chapter. In 1 Corinthians 12, Paul makes two major claims.

(1) The church has room for variety—indeed it should celebrate

its variety—but it has no room for distinctions. Even in the celebration of its variety, it acknowledges its basic unity, for the church has received one Spirit and it serves one Lord.

(2) The church is the body of Christ, not just metaphorically, but "really." As the body of Christ, the church—in all its variety—shows forth the brokenness, disgrace, and risk of the crucified Lord, as well as the presence, power, and teaching authority of the risen Lord.

Implications for the Teaching Church

We can now make explicit a number of implications of this chapter for the ministry of the teaching church.

The ministry of teaching is the ministry of the *whole* church. Since teaching is the business of recruiting and training citizens for the New Age, the whole community of the New Age is involved.

However, there are varieties of gifts which the church uses in its teaching ministry. The teaching ministry is not to be confined to the traditional educational structures of the church. Certainly the preaching clergy should be self-consciously involved in the teaching ministry. Preaching ministers should acknowledge that their function as preachers includes, necessarily, an educational role. They should self-consciously try to exercise that educational function effectively and faithfully. On the other side, all who are involved in the church's ministry should recognize that *Christian* education—like preaching—brings not just information, but also the power of the risen Lord to provide new life.

The worship service is to be seen as part of the church's teaching ministry—though, of course, not exclusively so. This is the time in the church's life when the whole church gathers together (including, of course, the children for part of the service). This is the place in the church's life where we act out our identity as the body of Christ. We act out our identity as Christ's body in part by being all together—young and old, of whatever race, educational background, or economic status. We act out our identity as the body of the crucified One by the openness and vulnerability with which we share one another's joys and sorrows, by the tender loving-kindness with which we reach out to one another. We act out our identity as the body of the risen One by the celebration of Christ's presence and power in the whole worship life of the church.

The church school should continue to play a central role in the church's educational ministry but not an isolated role. We should work together and accomplish by planning what my church once accomplished by luck—when the texts for the church school lesson and the sermon one Sunday morning were the same. The church school children heard the sermon with new openness and understanding, while the preacher had an unusually attentive congregation!

When the church exercises its teaching ministry in a variety of ways, even boards, committees, and clubs are part of the church's teaching ministry. They provide opportunities for self-conscious reflection on the church's life as the body of Christ. And they are often the places where church members see and decide what they really think the ministry of Christ's church can be. Nothing provides a better education in the church's self-understanding than those yearly meetings on the budget.

Further, the church should exercise its teaching ministry in the life of each member. Without undue self-consciousness, self-approbation, or guilt, members of the church should acknowledge that what they are is as much a part of the church's educational ministry as what the church school teaches or the preacher preaches.

Though the church rejoices in the great variety of its teaching ministry, it should rejoice equally in the fact that it is still a community without distinctions. It should resist any bragging or factionalism or divisiveness as it carries out its teaching ministry.

Each part of the church should want to strengthen the other parts of the church's teaching ministry. The church school should deliberately *not* compete with the morning worship—at least for young people and adults. The worship service should incorporate ideas and people from the church school.

The whole church should coordinate its ministry in working toward shared goals. The biblical injunction not to let our left hand know what our right hand is doing does not apply here. Our structures should enable, not hinder, that kind of shared planning which is essential to our life as the one body of Christ.

When the teaching church runs the risk of slipping into theological squabbling—especially over the issue of tongues, where the self-righteousness of one faction is often exceeded only by the anxiety of the other—we should remind ourselves that the great variety of our gifts is given by the same Spirit. In that Spirit, despite ourselves, we are still one.

Throughout our ministry we should remind ourselves that what we are given is a variety of service and not of privilege. We should remember that the legitimate question to be raised (as we gather in our subgroups to protect our bailiwicks) is not "How can we preserve our privileges?" but "How can we serve others?" We should remember that that is a legitimate question, even when the youth group wants to use the women's society's kitchen.

Because we are the body of Christ, we should acknowledge our interdependence. We should seek those forms of teaching which recognize the needs of younger people for older people and vice versa. We should seek to break down the dividing walls which often separate married people from single people, parents from childless people, or everybody from divorced or widowed people. We should even remember that one of the clearest forms of interdependence is the interdependence of teacher and student. In the body of Christ all are both teachers and learners.

Because we are the body of the crucified One, we should know that the usual standards of success and prestige are inadequate and finally unfaithful criteria for our ministry. We should ask what it is to face brokenness, disgrace, and risk as we minister to one another and minister to a needy world. Because we are the body of the risen One, we should trust not in our schemes but in his grace. We should entrust our weakness to his power. We should assume that in the midst of our poor teaching, Christ is still that Teacher who can and does bring new life to people and societies.

Perhaps most important, we should remember that the church best teaches by being the church. We should remember that the church best calls people to faith, hope, and love by being faithful, hopeful, and loving.

Precisely as we act as citizens of the New Age, we will enable others to see what the New Age is like. We will help them to decide for it or against it. Precisely as we are who we are, Christ's body, we will enable others to recognize that Christ whose body we are (however we may try to hide that fact). Though we know we have the treasure of the gospel in earthen vessels—real churches with actual boards, pastors, teachers, choirs, and members—yet what we have in earthen vessels is a treasure beyond all words to say. The teaching church receives that treasure with gratitude and shares it with joy.

Questions for Discussion

1. Why does Paul affirm the value of variety in the church?

2. How can we better affirm both the variety and the unity of our own congregation?

3. What does Paul mean when he calls the church "the body of Christ"?

4. What implications does Paul's vision of the church as Christ's body have for the teaching ministry of our own church?

3

How Does
the Church Teach?

The churches to which Paul wrote had some sense that they were communities of the New Age. They realized that as communities of the New Age they had a responsibility for teaching. However, as Paul heard about the way in which his churches had undertaken their teaching ministry, he was dissatisfied with the methods they used.

The Galatians (or at least some of them) thought that the purpose of the church's teaching ministry was to teach new Christians those rules which they were supposed to obey. The Galatian rule book was the Old Testament legal code, especially the rules about circumcision, the sabbath, and festivals. Paul, however, thinks that teaching lists of rules is a kind of education which was appropriate to the Old Age but which has no place in the New Age. Learning the law (the Torah) and obeying the law were the ways in which people tried to please God before God expressed God's good pleasure with people in Jesus Christ. Paul writes:

> Now before faith came [i.e., before the New Age came], we were confined under the law, kept under restraint until faith was revealed. So that the law was our custodian until Christ came, that we might be justified through faith. But now that faith has come, we are no longer under a custodian; for in Christ Jesus you are all children of God, through faith (Galatians 3:23-26, with some emendations of the author).

The Galatians tried to teach the rules and regulations of the Old Age. For Paul the purpose of teaching in the New Age is to open people to faith in Jesus Christ.

The Corinthians apparently had two different understandings of the church's teaching ministry, and Paul thinks that each of them is inadequate for the New Age.

One belief the Corinthians had was that the purpose of teaching is to impart to believers some kind of special knowledge. Christians are people who have received secret truths which no one outside the church can know. This kind of private information is that "wisdom" which we have already seen was so important to the Corinthians. Paul denies that the imparting of that kind of wisdom is appropriate to the church's teaching ministry. He quotes Scripture against the Corinthians:

> "I will destroy the wisdom of the wise,
> and the cleverness of the clever I will thwart."
> 1 Corinthians 1:19

Another belief the Corinthians had was that the purpose of instruction in the church is to enable Christians to realize that they are resurrected with Jesus. In our language, we might say that the purpose of Christian education is to enable people to feel that they have Jesus in their hearts. Now Paul certainly believes that life in the New Age is life in the presence of the risen Lord, but the Corinthians misunderstood the implications of that belief. Apparently, they thought that if they lived with the resurrected Lord, that in itself was a sufficient mark of the Christian life. The Christian life had no particular ethical or social implications. The Corinthians said: "It's the New Age, and we have Jesus in our hearts. That's all that matters, and anything goes."

Paul was terribly unhappy that the Corinthians failed to understand the ethical implications of life in the New Age; so he wrote to the Corinthians about one particularly blatant case of immorality which they were practicing:

> It is actually reported that there is immorality among you, and of a kind that is not found even among pagans; for a man is living with his father's wife. And you are arrogant! Ought you not rather to mourn? (1 Corinthians 5:1-2a).

Paul therefore insists, over against the Corinthians, that life in the New Age does not mean freedom from ethical responsibilities, though life in the New Age may allow us to see our ethical responsibilities in a new light.

We have our own versions of the Galatian and Corinthian views of teaching in our churches today.

Sometimes, like the Galatians, we try to teach the faith primarily as law, as a list of rules. We use the Bible as a kind of spiritual Ann Landers or Emily Post. The Bible supposedly contains the specific answers to every specific question of our personal and social lives. The purpose of Christian education is to teach Christians how to use the rule book effectively so that in every crisis of their lives they will be able to apply the appropriate law.

Sometimes, like the Corinthians, we think that the purpose of Christian education is to impart special and even secret wisdom. Our hope is that Christians will be able to recite the proper formulas of the faith. Our hope is that they will be able to say the secret words— whether or not they have any clear idea of what the words mean. Or our purpose is to help people memorize vast quantities of knowledge—Bible facts or Bible verses—without raising the crucial question: How do those facts or those verses affect and inform our lives? (At one church where I served, the members of the church school prided themselves on the fact that they could recite the books of the Bible backwards. This display of esoteric knowledge was a matter of some wonderment and little value.)

Or again, like the Corinthians, we think that the purpose of our educational ministry is to allow people to be right with Jesus or to have Jesus in their hearts. We rightly think that the point of our teaching is to enable people to live in the New Age, but we wrongly forget that citizenship in the New Age carries with it particular obligations and responsibilities. This misunderstanding of our teaching takes two forms.

The "conservative" form suggests that as long as we have a close, personal relationship to Jesus, we don't need to figure out the implications of that relationship for our business practices. We certainly don't have to figure out the implications of that relationship for the way we vote, use our purchasing power, or engage in the "dirty" work of politics.

The "progressive" form of the Corinthian misunderstanding suggests that as long as we can engage in warm and open relationships, as long as we have learned to be loving persons, we don't need guidelines for the Christian life. We can just do what comes naturally, leaving aside such old-fashioned issues as responsibility.

Undoubtedly, there is some truth in each of these understandings of the church's mode of teaching. However, none of them is adequate to Paul's vision of the church as a community of the New Age or to his picture of the church's role as teacher.

For the remainder of this chapter we shall look at four ways in which Paul teaches, and we shall suggest that these provide helpful guidelines for the way in which we can teach in our own churches.

Paul's four ways of teaching are these:

(1) Paul uses *tradition,* in the hope that the churches will *remember.*

(2) Paul uses *proclamation,* in the hope that the churches will *hear.*

(3) Paul uses *exhortation,* in the hope that the churches will *obey.*

(4) Paul uses *imitation,* in the hope that the churches will *imitate.*

Paul's Use of Tradition as a Means of Teaching

In the first chapter of the letter to the Galatians, Paul insists that he did not receive the gospel from any person but received it directly from the Lord:

> For I would have you know, brethren, that the gospel which was preached by me is not man's gospel. For I did not receive it from man, nor was I taught it, but it came through a revelation of Jesus Christ (Galatians 1:11-12).

Most of us are not so fortunate. The gospel we receive has not come to us through a direct revelation of Jesus Christ. It has come to us through the mediation of other people. Apart from them and the tradition they have shared with us, we should never have believed.

Even Paul, at two crucial points in his first letter to the Corinthians, writes of the tradition which he has received from others as an important part of his own learning and teaching.

One of these passages is 1 Corinthians 15:3-7:

> For I delivered to you as of first importance what I also received, that Christ died for our sins in accordance with the scriptures, that he was buried, that he was raised on the third day in accordance with the scriptures, and that he appeared to Cephas [Peter] . . . [Paul then goes on to recite a list of other resurrection appearances].

Several features of this passage help us to understand Paul's use of tradition in his teaching.

The terms "received" and "delivered" in the first sentence of this passage are terms which the rabbis used when they spoke of passing on from generation to generation that oral tradition which was the heart of their teaching. Here, Paul places himself in the line of those faithful teachers who have interpreted God's will from age to age by passing on the traditions of the faith by word of mouth.

What Paul passes on, the tradition which he delivers, consists of both a list of historical facts and a series of theological interpretations of those facts. This combination of claims about facts and interpretations of those facts in the light of faith is altogether typical of the early teaching and preaching of the Christian church.[1]

The facts which Paul cites here include these: Jesus died; Jesus was buried; Jesus appeared to Peter and various other people presumably known to the Corinthians.

However, the statements of fact are interpreted in the light of a faith which is much richer and more suggestive than the facts alone. Christ died *"for our sins"* and *"in accordance with the scriptures."* The death of Jesus had a particular purpose, and that purpose has to do with us and our redemption from sin. Furthermore, the death of Jesus was foretold in the Old Testament, which means that faithful people will recognize in Jesus' death the gracious and mysterious purpose of that God who speaks through the Old Testament.

Jesus *"was raised."* This gives a theological explanation of the fact of the resurrection appearances. For a Jew, the use of the passive "Jesus *was raised*" is a way of speaking of God's activity without directly naming God. Paul here gives a theological explanation for the resurrection appearances. God raised Jesus. This resurrection, too, is "in accordance with the scriptures." The faithful person can see in the resurrection the gracious purpose and foreknowledge of God.

This is the mark of Christian tradition from the very beginning until now. We don't just pass on a set of facts:

> Jesus was born in Bethlehem,
> ministered in Galilee,
> died in Jerusalem,
> and on the third day they found an empty tomb,
> and some people claimed that they saw Jesus.

We also pass on a faithful (faith-full), theological interpretation of those facts:

God sent Jesus, the Messiah, God's Son, who was born in David's city, Bethlehem.

Jesus proclaimed and acted out the kingdom of God in Galilee.

He died for our sins in Jerusalem.

And on the third day God raised him from the dead so that through him we might have eternal life.

The other passage where Paul makes extensive reference to tradition is 1 Corinthians 11:23-25:

> For I received from the Lord what I also delivered to you, that the Lord Jesus on the night when he was betrayed took bread, and when he had given thanks, he broke it, and said, "This is my body which is [broken] for you. Do this in remembrance of me." In the same way also the cup, after supper, saying, "This cup is the new covenant in my blood. Do this, as often as you drink it, in remembrance of me."

There are three features of this passage which help us further understand Paul's use of tradition.

For one thing, Paul again uses the terms for "receiving" and "delivering" the oral tradition. Here, however, he says that he received the tradition of the Supper *from the Lord*. Now, presumably Paul doesn't mean that during the Damascus Road experience or some later ecstatic occasion, the risen Lord gave him a brief indoctrination on the words of institution for the Last Supper (especially since the tradition Paul cites here is so close to the tradition we find in the Synoptic Gospels). What Paul means is that he has received this tradition from other Christians. Yet his receiving of the tradition from other Christians is a way of receiving it from the Lord. For Paul, the Lord sometimes speaks to him precisely through that tradition which other Christians pass on. (Presumably, that gives us a clue to the importance of Scripture in our own tradition. Scripture contains the Word of the Lord, not because the Holy Spirit dictated every word into the ears of passive scribes, but because Scripture is the way in which the church passes on the traditions about Jesus from generation to generation.)

For another thing, the tradition which Paul has received doesn't just provide information; it calls for action. According to this tradition, Christians aren't just told to learn things; they are called to do things. *"Do this* in remembrance of me." *"Do this,* as often as you drink it, in remembrance of me." For Paul, one way of learning the tradition is to act it out, to relive it. In that way the tradition becomes part of the lives of believers. Or put another way, for Paul tradition is not just something to be understood; it is something to be lived. If we really learn the tradition of the Last Supper, we live in a certain way.

Finally, the point of hearing the tradition, learning the tradition, is *remembrance:* "Do this in *remembrance* of me." Remembrance in the New Testament does not mean, as we often think, just a polite, nostalgic nod to the past. The Lord's Supper to which Paul called the Corinthians is not (as in some of our churches) a quiet memorial service for a late, lamented Lord.

We find another use of the word for remembering in the story of the two criminals in Luke's Gospel. The faithful criminal says to Jesus: "Jesus, *remember* me when you come into your [kingly power]" (Luke 23:42, author's italics). The criminal is clearly not saying that when the kingdom comes, Jesus is supposed to pause, think kindly of that poor dead criminal, and then go about his kingly business. The criminal means that when Jesus comes as King, Jesus is to make him present, bring him into the kingdom, too.

So for Paul, Jesus' words "Do this in remembrance of me" mean "Do this in order to make me present among you." By rightly remembering and acting out the story of the Last Supper, we don't just look back on poor dead Jesus. We celebrate, enact, entice the presence of the living Lord.

So, too, whenever the traditions of the faith become *our* traditions, the past becomes present for us. The story of our fathers and mothers in the faith becomes our story. As we act out the biblical history, it becomes our history.

We catch this kind of "remembrance" better in our songs than we do in most of our life as a church. Note the words of the spiritual:

When Israel was in Egypt's land, [as if that were only a past circumstance]
Let my people go! [beginning to make the story *our* story]
Oppressed so hard they could not stand, [still past]
Let my people go!
Go down, Moses,'Way down in Egypt's land,
Tell old Pharaoh, "Let my people go!"

Now, in the refrain, the story has become our story. The past has become our present. *We* are beseeching Moses on our behalf to intercede with Pharaoh. It is our liberation which we seek.

Whenever we rightly remember the tradition, the past becomes present. The words of the Scripture become words about us. The Lord whom we remember is present in our midst.

Paul's Use of Proclamation as a Means of Teaching

The second mode of teaching which Paul employs is proclamation. For Paul, as for us, proclamation primarily means preaching. However, he does not confine the ministry of proclamation to one hour on Sunday morning nor to a group of professional preachers. Proclamation is one of the gifts which God gives to various people in the church. For Paul proclamation is perhaps the heart of the church's ministry. Certainly it is an essential part of the church's role as teacher, especially as the church carries on its mission of recruiting citizens for the New Age.

Paul's fullest discussion of the role of proclamation in the church is found in 1 Corinthians 1–2.

Paul writes first about *what* is proclaimed. What is the content of our preaching, our witnessing? (Remember that Paul here writes to a congregation which is enamored of secret wisdom, as if that wisdom were central to the gospel.)

> For since, in the wisdom of God, the world did not know God through wisdom, it pleased God through the folly of what we preach to save those who believe. For Jews demand signs and Greeks seek wisdom, but we preach Christ crucified, a stumbling block to Jews and folly to Gentiles, but to those who are called, both Jews and Greeks, Christ the power of God and the wisdom of God. For the foolishness of God is wiser than men, and the weakness of God is stronger than men (1 Corinthians 1:21-25).

For Paul the content of our preaching is always and only Jesus Christ—and Jesus Christ crucified. A story is told of a church in a little seaport town in the south of Sweden. One Sunday in 1716, the great warrior-hero-king Charles XII visited this little congregation. This visit was not expected by the pastor, and he was so overwhelmed that instead of preaching his prepared sermon, he substituted an ardent eulogy of the king and the royal family. A few months later, the church received a gift from King Charles. It was a crucifix. Included with the gift were these instructions: "This is to hang on the pillar opposite the pulpit so that all who shall stand there will be reminded of their proper subject."[2]

That pastor, of course, only demonstrated what was true in Paul's time and is true in our own. It is very difficult and painful to focus our preaching, our proclamation, on the cross.

The cross *is* a sign of foolishness. It is hard for us (as for the Corinthians) to proclaim the cross precisely when we are trying to show how wise it is to accept the Christian faith. The problem is that the cross finally doesn't fit all those careful, intellectual categories by which we try to analyze the shape of the world and the needs of persons. The problem is that the cross doesn't even fit all our prudential calculations about how to find happiness and significance in our own lives. There is something foolish about the idea that God's love for all humankind has been acted out at a place of execution. In the light of that claim, we have to revise our categories, rethink our goals, reinterpret our needs. That kind of reinterpretation of conventional wisdom is always painful, and we have to acknowledge that.

The cross *is* a sign of weakness. The cross stands against all the idols of a people and a nation eager for power. The cross stands against the modest claims we make for personal power or for power for our churches. The cross stands against our attempts to show that Christianity promises success and prosperity either for ourselves or for our congregations. The cross even stands against the hope that as Christians we should be able to exert much influence on the ways of the world. The cross stands against our false pride in our false self-sufficiency. The cross always recalls us to the word Paul received from the Lord: "My grace is sufficient for you, for my power is made perfect in weakness" (2 Corinthians 12:9*a*).

Over against all the standards of the Old Age—the pride in wisdom and the lust for power—we proclaim the sign of the New Age: the cross. We proclaim God's foolishness and God's weakness which have brought about a new creation.

Paul writes not only of *what* we proclaim but of *how* we proclaim:

> When I came to you, brethren, I did not come proclaiming to you the testimony of God in lofty words or wisdom. For I decided to know nothing among you except Jesus Christ and him crucified. And I was with you in weakness and in much fear and trembling; and my speech and my message were not in plausible words of wisdom, but in demonstration of the Spirit and of power, that your faith might not rest in the wisdom of men but in the power of God (1 Corinthians 2:1-5).

Those of us who are preachers (or who listen to preachers) are sometimes convinced that in the good old days preaching had an eloquence, authority, and self-evident power which ours lacks. We feel sorry for ourselves because we find ourselves competing with television—which is far more entertaining than we. Or we find ourselves competing with university lecturers who are far more enlightening than we.

Yet Paul here indicates that he was no paragon as an entertainer or enlightener, either. For Paul the *form* of preaching corresponds to the *content* of preaching. We proclaim that in the foolishness and weakness of the cross God has shown forth God's power. We discover that even in the foolishness and weakness of our preaching God continues to show forth God's power. God can use the inadequacy and implausibility of our preaching to bring the enlivening word of grace.

(Needless to say, this strong reliance on God's grace does not give the contemporary preacher license to specialize in inarticulate implausibility. That is the "preacherly" version of the old heresy: "What . . . then? Are we to continue in sin that grace may abound?" [Romans 6:1]. To which Paul, exasperated, replies: "God forbid!" This understanding or preaching does, however, provide comfort when we have done the best we know how to do and realize that our best comes nowhere near the majesty of the gospel we proclaim.)

In the light of Paul's understanding of preaching, we can rightly be skeptical of the frantic search to find new and clever gimmicks to keep the art of preaching alive. We live under the promise that if we preach faithfully—if we really proclaim Christ crucified—God can and will bring life even through the weakness and foolishness of our preaching.

Further, Paul writes of how we receive the proclamation. He writes of the goal of that proclamation. Here we move from Corinthians to Galatians: "Let me ask you only this: Did you receive the Spirit by works of the law, or by hearing with faith?" (Galatians 3:2).

The mark of the Old Age was doing works of the law. People tried to win or coerce the presence of the Spirit by the things they did. They worked desperately to prove their credentials so that God would be gracious to them.

In one sense, life in the New Age is much more passive. Instead of working to win God's presence, we sit still and *hear* the Good News of God's presence. We *receive* the gift of God's presence—God's Spirit—through faith.[3]

This verse in Galatians gives one answer to the question of the purpose of our proclamation: What do we want people to do in response to our proclamation or preaching? The answer is that we want them to *hear* the Good News which we preach. We want them really to hear it. We want them to be able to say, "That word is a word about me." The ability to accept the word as a word about oneself is part of what Paul means by faith. That faithful hearing is the goal of our ministry of proclamation.

Paul's Use of Exhortation as a Means of Teaching

One of the best-known passages of Pauline teaching is Romans 12:1-2:

> I exhort you, therefore, brethren, by the mercies of God, to present your bodies as a living sacrifice, holy and acceptable to God, which is your spiritual worship. Do not be conformed to this age, but be transformed by having your minds made new, so that you may prove what is the will of God, what is good and acceptable and perfect (emended by the author).

This ethical exhortation shows that Paul's basic moral concern is precisely the concern with how Christians live as citizens of the New Age. Christians are not to be conformed to "this age," i.e., to the Old Age which is passing away. Their minds are to be "made new" so that they are "transformed" and become part of the new creation, the New Age which is established in Jesus Christ. The way one lives in the New Age is to prove, or discover, or work out "what is the will of God." The New Age is the age which is wholly ruled by God's sovereign will. Citizenship in that age requires discovering and living according to that will.

The opening word of the passage sets the tone for Paul's ethical teaching: "I exhort" (Greek, *parakalō).* Paul often uses this word at the beginning of one of his sections of ethical instruction, and it indicates the mood of that instruction even when he doesn't use the term explicitly. The term has two implications which help us understand Paul's ethical teaching—and our own.

For one thing, the term connotes a kind of urgency. Paul doesn't merely suggest or recommend. He exhorts, or beseeches, or begs, or urges, or makes an appeal. For Paul, as for us, the ethical dimension of the Christian faith isn't simply an inconsequential afterthought to the gospel. It is a necessary consequence of the gospel. Like the gospel, it is a matter of utmost urgency.

For another thing, the term "I exhort" implies that the life of the teacher is involved in the life of the student; the life of the apostle is tied up with the life of his churches. When I say to you, "I beg you to act in such and such a way," that is very different from saying, "I suggest that you act in such and such a way," or "I recommend that you act in such and such a way." When I beg you to do something, I admit that I'm personally involved in the request. What you do makes a difference not just to you but to me, too. When Paul exhorts, begs his churches to behave in a certain way, he admits that their behavior makes an immense difference to him. His life, not just their own, is at stake in their behavior. So, too, when our churches engage in ethical instruction, we don't do so from a disinterested distance. We exhort one another in the Christian life precisely because we are intimately involved with one another. The growth of one Christian in the duties and responsibilities of the faith enriches us all. The irresponsibility of any Christian diminishes us all. In other words, Christian ethical teaching requires a community of love in which the "instructor" and the "instructed" are bound together in a common concern.

Paul uses this teaching as exhortation to touch on a wide variety of implications of the Christian life. Indeed, a typically diverse group of concerns comes under the initial "I exhort you" of Romans 12:1. Paul goes on to give the Romans instructions on

> how to get along with one another in church (Romans 12:3-13);
>
> how to get along with persecutors and enemies (12:14-21);
>
> how to relate to political authorities (13:1-7);
>
> the value of love (13:8-10);
>
> the dangers of drunkenness and debauchery (13:11-14);
>
> and how to get along with vegetarians and Sabbatarians (14:1-23).

Clearly Paul does not make the mistake which the Corinthians made. He does not think that citizenship in the New Age relieves Christians of moral obligations. On the contrary, citizenship in the New Age has implications for all our everyday activities and relationships. That is why Paul's letters include so much exhortation.

Paul's exhortation relies on three kinds of warrants. The three kinds of reasons he uses for his ethical instructions can also help us in the church's ministry of exhortation.

First, Paul uses the warrant of *Jesus' own teachings.* Paul does not use this warrant very often. This may be because he was not aware of as much of Jesus' teaching as we are. (He had not read the Gospels.) Or it may be that he was aware of Jesus' teaching but did not think it as important a guide to ethical action as we do.

However, as we have seen, there is at least one point where Paul refers to a teaching of the earthly Jesus as a reason for his ethical instruction. In 1 Corinthians 7:10-11 he is writing the Corinthians on the question of divorce: "To the married I give charge, not I but the Lord, that the wife should not separate from her husband (but if she does, let her remain single or else be reconciled to her husband)—and that the husband should not divorce his wife."

This is a clear reference to the saying of Jesus which we find in Mark 10:2ff. and in Matthew 19:3ff. Here, therefore, Paul does take Jesus' word as an authoritative ethical guide (cf. also Romans 12:14; 13:8).

Second, more often Paul bases his ethical instructions on larger theological principles. That is, his understanding of the Christian ethical life isn't based on a series of Jesus' explicit teachings. His understanding of the Christian ethical life is based on his understanding of the whole meaning of Jesus' incarnation, death, and resurrection. Jesus' significance as God's gift of love for humankind provides the basis for Paul's ethical reflections.

The connection between theological principles and ethical implications permeates Paul's writing. The mundane and the spiritual are closely interwoven. Perhaps more accurately, Paul does not make the distinctions we do between the mundane and the spiritual.

When Paul urges the Corinthians to do their part in the offering for Jerusalem, he bases that appeal on their faith in the incarnation:

> I say this not as a command, but to prove by the earnestness of others that your love also is genuine. For you know the grace of our Lord Jesus Christ, that though he was rich, yet for your sake he became poor, so that by his poverty you might become rich (2 Corinthians 8:8-9).

When Paul urges the Romans to accept vegetarians and Sabbatarians lovingly, he deals with the practical problem of getting along with each other on the basis of his whole understanding of Christ's death and resurrection:

> One man esteems one day as better than another, while another man esteems all days alike. Let every one be fully convinced in his own mind. He who observes the day, observes it in honor of the Lord. He also who eats, eats in honor of the Lord, since he gives thanks to God; while he who abstains, abstains in honor of the Lord and gives thanks to God. None of us lives to himself, and none of us dies to himself. If we live, we live to the Lord, and if we die, we die to the Lord; so then, whether we live or whether we die, we are the Lord's. For to this end Christ died and lived again, that he might be Lord both of the dead and of the living (Romans 14:5-9).

Notice that Paul's way of talking about ethics is not usually to use proof texts, whether from the teaching of Jesus or from the Old Testament (which was Paul's Bible). Paul's way of teaching ethics is usually more complicated than that. He moves from a concrete, practical situation to his understanding of the whole economy of God's dealing with humankind in Jesus Christ and then back again.

This surely has implications for the ethical teaching of our churches. It is all too easy for us to try to hit each other over the head with proof texts. It is much more difficult—and much more faithful—to try to understand the whole context of God's love for us as we see it in Jesus Christ and to move from that understanding to draw practical implications for our ethical life.

Third, Paul sometimes does his ethical teaching on the basis of what can best be described as common sense.[4] For example, in 1 Corinthians 7, after Paul has spoken against divorce on the basis of a teaching of Jesus, he goes on to write:

> Now concerning the unmarried, I have no command of the Lord, but I give *my opinion* as one who by the Lord's mercy is trustworthy (1 Corinthians 7:25, author's italics).

Paul is not afraid, as part of his ethical instruction, simply to give his opinion as one Christian person trying honestly and intelligently to live an ethical life.

In a similar way, in the long discussion on speaking in tongues, in 1 Corinthians 12–14, Paul not only uses careful theological arguments, but he also points out that *practically* the stress on tongues in worship simply doesn't do much good:

> If, therefore, the whole church assembles and all speak in tongues, and outsiders or unbelievers enter, will they not say that you are mad? (1 Corinthians 14:23).

The clearest statement of Paul's reliance on simple good sense comes earlier in the first letter to the Corinthians. The Corinthians had apparently picked up on Paul's belief that Christ is the end of the law and had interpreted that belief to mean that anything goes. Paul responded to this theological misinterpretation not with more theology but with a prime example of common sense:

> [You say] "All things are lawful for me," but [says Paul] not all things are helpful (1 Corinthians 6:12*a*).

Again, Paul's willingness to use common sense suggests that at some points we can share with each other, not on the basis of advanced theological reflection, but on the basis of our experience as human beings. One of my professors once preached a chapel sermon on the problem of sexual promiscuity. Having nodded to the theological dimensions of the problem, he spent most of the sermon reciting statistics on venereal disease and unexpected pregnancies and ended by saying: "In a word, promiscuity is stupid." The sermon had an impact beyond the subtlety of its scriptural exposition, and in Paul's terms it was a legitimate kind of Christian exhortation.

If the goal of teaching by tradition is remembrance and the goal of teaching by proclamation is hearing, then the goal of teaching by exhortation is obedience. The goal is not obedience to the teacher, of course, since the teacher has no authority of his or her own. The goal is obedience to that will of God which is the principle by which we live life in the New Age. It is not dumb obedience or blind obedience. It is obedience which includes the hard work of trying to discern, to "prove" God's will in changing situations. It is obedience which is sensitive to the commands of Christ as we understand them. It is obedience which seeks to apply the Good News of God's love in Jesus Christ to a variety of concrete, practical situations. It is obedience which is not afraid to rely on common sense, believing that our brains and society's experience are also gifts of the Creator God. It is obedience which is directed, finally, not to any book, set of rules, or institution, but to the living Lord who has spoken, does speak, and will speak among us. That is why when Paul writes explicitly of the church's teaching ministry, he says:

> But thanks be to God, that you who were once slaves of sin have become obedient from the heart to the standard of teaching to which you were committed, and, having been set free from sin, have become slaves of righteousness. But now that you have been set free from sin and have become slaves of God, the return you get is sanctification and its end, eternal life (Romans 6:17-18, 22).

Paul's Use of Imitation as a Means of Teaching

One of Paul's more striking suggestions to the Corinthians is found in 1 Corinthians 10:31–11:1:

> So, whether you eat or drink, or whatever you do, do all to the glory of God. Give no offense to Jews or to Greeks or to the church of God, just as I try to please all men in everything I do, not seeking my own advantage, but that of many, that they may be saved. Be imitators of me, as I am of Christ.

Here Paul uses the teaching device of imitation. He urges the Corinthians to follow his example.

He does not urge Christians to imitate Christ (but see 1 Thessalonians 1:6). That is probably just as well since, after all, Jesus was God's Chosen One and we are the ones he came to redeem. Jesus is our Lord, and we are his people. There is something audacious, if not arrogant, about thinking that we are called to imitate Jesus in any explicit way. Paul, of course, claims that he *does* imitate Jesus; but Paul never suffers from undue modesty. And if anyone has a right to claim that in his zeal and his suffering he imitates the Lord, it is Paul and not we.

There are several ways in which Paul urges Christians to imitate himself. In each of these instances we can see why teaching by imitation is more effective and more faithful than simply teaching by words.

First, Paul urges Christians to imitate his loving-kindness in their relations with one another:

> I do not write this to make you ashamed, but to admonish you as my beloved children. For though you have countless guides in Christ, you do not have many fathers. For I became your father in Christ Jesus through the gospel. I urge you, then, be imitators of me (1 Corinthians 4:14-16).

Paul here sees the essential point that it is not enough to encourage loving-kindness among the Corinthians unless he himself has shown loving-kindness to them. He doesn't stand outside the community and impose on the Christians an alien law of love. He points them to the life which they have shared in common with him, and he finds in that common life the picture of the love he desires.

So, too, in the passage we have already quoted from 1 Corinthians 10:31–11:1 Paul calls the Corinthians "not to seek their own advantage." This is a call precisely to that love which recognizes no distinctions within the church, and Paul is able to point to his own conduct as a Christian person who acknowledges no distinctions in the body of Christ.

Second, Paul urges Christians to imitate him by sharing even in the suffering which comes from faithfulness to the gospel. So he writes to the Thessalonians:

> And you became imitators of us and of the Lord, for you received the word in much affliction, with joy inspired by the Holy Spirit; so that you became an example to all the believers in Macedonia and in Achaia (1 Thessalonians 1:6-7).

Paul throughout his ministry does imitate Christ in his willingness to suffer persecution for the sake of the gospel. He believes that just as the power of God brought the resurrection triumph out of the suffering of Good Friday, so God's power in Christ can use Paul's suffering to work toward redemption for the world. So, after a long list of his sufferings and losses, Paul writes:

> For the sake of Christ, then, I am content with weaknesses, insults, hardships, persecutions, and calamities; for when I am weak, then I am strong (2 Corinthians 12:10).[5]

In the passage from First Thessalonians, Paul commends the Thessalonians on following the same pattern. For them, too, the gospel has meant both affliction and joy, both weakness and power. In their willingness to suffer affliction for the sake of the gospel, they imitate Paul, who imitates Christ.

Again, Paul does not call Christians to a sacrifice which he does not share. He is not an armchair general, sitting far behind the front lines and urging others to take risks he will not dare. He is not a comfortable Christian who finds in the gospel the requirement that others should make sacrifices but who never makes sacrifices himself. Surely he is right in seeing that when teaching involves the call to suffering, only the teacher who has known suffering can make that demand of others.

Third—and this is only implicit in Paul's letters—Christians can imitate Paul's deep human involvement in what he teaches. In Paul's letters—with all their odd mixture of ego and humility, grumpiness and grace—there is never any question that Paul is wholly *there* in what he teaches. The gospel he proclaims is the gospel which judges and redeems his own life, and there is no separation between the principles he proclaims and the life he tries to live.

Here, above all, Paul may provide an example for the church and its teachers. Surely the fullness of our humanity (not just our official piety) must be present in what we teach. What we hope others will imitate is not the particular style of our life or even the particular dogmas by which we live. What we hope others will imitate is the fact that the gospel has become Good News *to us.* What we hope we can show forth is the fact that we stake our lives, in all their mix of weakness and strength, on the gospel which we teach.

For Paul, the goal of teaching by imitation is imitation. Paul hopes that when he sets an example for his churches, they will follow his example. Of course, he doesn't really hope that they will be little

Pauls—saying just what he says or doing just what he does. That kind of imitation is slavery. What he does hope is that they will hear the word of the gospel in such a way that they will be freed to be loving, as he seeks to be loving; they will be freed to make sacrifices, as he makes sacrifices; they will be freed to be human, as he is human, bringing their full humanity to the service of Christ.

A cautionary note needs to be added. One thing that bothers many people about Paul is that he seems to be *too* self-consciously aware that others are looking at him. (Or at least he keeps hoping that others are looking.) In his refusal to boast of his strength, he perhaps too easily becomes proud of his "weakness." He is too self-conscious in his faithfulness. Of course, if Paul *were* to boast (as he himself would admit), he would have a good deal to boast about. Presumably, we have far less. Our faithfulness and our zeal—even on our best days—are poor shadows of his. So while we can acknowledge from time to time that we teach in part by imitation, we had probably best not dwell on that thought for long. It tends to make us focus too proudly on our own goodness or too despairingly on our own failing. It tends to start us searching for credentials again. Most of the time we should focus our confidence where it belongs—on the saving mercy of God—and leave the business of imitation to take care of itself.

Implications for the Teaching Church

We can now review the four ways in which Paul teaches and see more concretely how these provide guides to the church's teaching today.

First, Paul teaches by means of tradition. The purpose of this teaching is to encourage remembrance. This suggests that for our churches, too, there is no escape from the past. There is no escape from the Bible, no escape from church history, no escape from the stories which help to form our faith. The teaching church must always be involved in passing on those traditions, those stories, which shape our lives as a church.

However, we must not be concerned only with memorizing the stories but also with *remembering* them (in the sense that Paul speaks of remembering). We must enact the stories; we must "do this" in remembrance of Christ and of God's other faithful people. The questions which face us as a church which teaches tradition are these: How do we tell and act out the stories of the faith so that they become our stories? How do we appropriate "ancient history" in such a way that it makes a clear difference in our own lives and the life of our congregation? How do we interpret the "facts" of the stories in such a way that they entice faith in the hearers? (We cannot simply assume that the old interpretations of the facts will always entice faith despite our changing circumstances. The fact that Jesus died and rose again does not change; the ways of appropriating those facts to our own faith may change.)

Second, Paul teaches by means of proclamation. This means that for Paul, at least, the sermon or the witnessing ministry of the church is the most important kind of teaching. Whether we accept that or not, we shall want to acknowledge that preaching or proclamation is one crucial way in which the church does teach.

More than that, we must insist that the whole life of the church— the church school, the worship service, social activities, community action—should include this element of proclamation. We must have as the focus for our whole ministry Jesus Christ and him crucified. We must remember, in our whole ministry, that the gospel is always apt to come in foolishness and weakness. Therefore, while we try to have large and successful programs, we must remember that small and marginal programs can also be the means of God's grace.

We must remember that God's promise is to use the weakness of our preaching to show forth God's power. While we are certainly open to new modes of preaching, we must not assume that we can compete with television in titillating our congregation. Our first task must still be rightly to discern God's Word and faithfully to apply God's Word to the needs of people. Our abiding conviction must be that God is present in such preaching.

The teaching ministry of our churches must seek to move people toward the point where they can really *hear* the saving word of the proclamation: God in Jesus Christ loves you. We know that when people really hear that word as a word about themselves, lives are changed, worlds are changed. There is a new creation.

Third, Paul teaches by means of exhortation. Like Paul, our teaching churches must insist that the Christian faith, citizenship in the New Age, has immensely vital ethical implications.

Sometimes we must seek to understand those ethical implications by a straightforward appeal to the words of Jesus or to other pertinent Scripture.

Far more often, however, we need to move beyond ethical proof texting to try to understand the larger theological principles on the basis of which we can make our ethical decisions. We must want to understand as clearly as we can the implications of our faith in Christ's incarnation, death, and resurrection for the hard issues of our time. Certainly this mode of ethical reflection will be far more helpful to us than simply quoting Scripture when we discuss such issues as medical ethics, the role of women in the church, the place of gay people in church and society, or the relationship of the Christian to the nation.

When we as the church teach by means of ethical exhortation, we must not be ashamed of using common sense, secular knowledge, or scientific insight to help us in our moral reasoning. We can affirm that common sense, secular knowledge, and scientific insights are also gifts of God.

When we teach by means of exhortation, we must seek, like Paul, to convey the urgency of what we teach. More than that, like Paul, we must remember that no great gap divides those who exhort from those who are exhorted. We search *with one another* for the shape of the responsible Christian life, because we are bound together in love and in the commitment to grow together as members of the body of Christ. Therefore, we must be wary of any form of ethical instruction which presumes that some Christians are moral superstars who can simply issue pronouncements from the height of their wisdom and not from the depth of their caring.

The goal of our ministry of exhortation must not be merely understanding but obedience. Our goal, of course, must not be obedience to any human authority—neither a pastor, nor a teacher, nor a board, nor the church itself. Our goal must be obedience to the living Lord. Our hope will be that on the basis of our exhortation we will not only think differently, but we will live differently as well.

Fourth, Paul teaches by means of imitation. The danger, of course, with teaching by imitation is that we will do it self-consciously. We will keep looking over our shoulder to see whether anyone is noticing how wonderfully Christian we are.

On the other hand, all of us know that that kind of teaching by example, imitation, is a central part of the church's teaching ministry. All of us can bear witness to those Christians who may never have taught us anything by what they said but who showed us the richness of the faith precisely by who they were.

We also know that the call to love by an unloving person is a call which is very hard to hear. We know that the demand for sacrifice by a comfortable Christian is easily ignored. We know that the words of faith are most compelling when they are spoken by a person whose life, in all its mix of good and ill, is wholly present in the words.

We know that those of us who are teachers need at least to continue to *hope* that our lives sometimes show forth the faith and hope and love we teach. And we can pray that God will use the imperfection of our faith and hope and love to do more than we can— or should—ever know or imagine.

Finally, we can suggest that these four modes of teaching correspond to the marks which we saw are indicative of the church's life.

The church is the community without credentials. The appropriate mode of teaching for such a community is proclamation. Proclamation preaches the Good News that we are loved by sheer grace and not because of our credentials or because of anything we do. Proclamation is not received by anything we do but by simply hearing, through faith.

The church is the community without distinctions. The appropriate mode of teaching for such a community is exhortation. Exhortation itself breaks down the division between teacher and student. Both teacher and student are involved in ethical growth and responsibility. The content of exhortation is precisely the ethical responsibility of treating the neighbor as the self, of not vaunting our rights at the expense of others.

The church is the community without end. The appropriate mode of teaching for such a. community is tradition. In the community without end we make the stories of our fathers and mothers in the faith alive for ourselves, and we pass them on to our children.

Imitation is the way in which we live out what we teach. By imitation we not only speak but also act as Paul did. We live as true citizens of the new community—the community without credentials, or distinctions, or end.

Questions for Discussion

1. What is the place of *remembering* in Paul's writings? What is the place of remembering in our own church's teaching ministry?

2. How can we proclaim the centrality of the cross of Jesus in our church?

3. What does Paul see as the importance of ethical responsibility in the New Age? How can our church best teach ethical responsibilities?

4. What are the dangers and the values of teaching by example?

4

What Does the Church Teach? 1. Faith

For Paul, life in the New Age is life which is marked by two great gifts—faith and love: "For in Christ Jesus neither circumcision nor uncircumcision is of any avail, but faith working through love" (Galatians 5:6). Therefore, the church, as the community of the New Age, is committed to teach its recruits and its members both faith and love. In this chapter we shall try to understand what Paul means by "faith"; and in the next chapter we shall try to understand how that faith works, or is made active, through "love."

Before Faith—the Law

From the beginning of his ministry Paul faced an enormous pastoral problem. What was he to preach and teach Gentile Christians? The earliest Christians had, of course, been Jews; and as long as they were preaching the gospel to other Jews, there was no problem with what to do about the law. Those who preached the gospel obeyed the Jewish law. They assumed that those who were converted by the gospel would also obey the Jewish law.

However, even before Paul was converted, some Christians began to preach the gospel to non-Jews; and this posed a problem for the church. Would the Christians require Gentile converts to keep the

Jewish law as well? After all, new Christians were expected to accept the Old Testament as their Bible. Didn't it make sense to assume that they would also be expected to keep dietary laws, to have their males circumcised, and to behave as good Jews?

It is not altogether clear which early church leaders thought that all Christian converts should keep the Jewish law. There is some evidence in the first two chapters of Galatians that James, the brother of Jesus, held such a view and that Peter vacillated on the issue. What is clear is that Paul joined that group of Christians who held that Gentiles should not be required to keep the Jewish law in order to become Christians. Indeed, he thought that the stress on the law was diametrically opposed to the gospel which he preached.

Therefore, when he writes Galatians, Paul is extremely upset. He has learned that some opponents have come to the Galatian churches and have tried to persuade the men of the churches that they must be circumcised and all the members of the churches that they must keep the sabbath and other Jewish festivals.

Since the Galatians have been beguiled by these exponents of the Old Testament law, Paul decides to fight fire with fire—to fight their interpretation of the Old Testament with his own.

Probably drawing on some rabbinic commentaries on the Book of Genesis, Paul turns to the figure of Abraham to make his argument. Abraham is a useful figure for Paul because, like the Gentiles, Abraham stood outside the law. The Gentiles stand outside the law because they are not part of the Sinai covenant. Abraham stood outside the law because he lived prior to the Sinai covenant. Yet, clearly Abraham was a great model of a life blessed and approved by God.

When Paul turns to the story of Abraham, he uses a text which becomes the keystone for his argument with the Galatians. In Genesis 15, God promises Abraham that he will have a son despite his old age and that through his son he will have many descendants. The text says: "Abraham 'had faith in God, and it was accounted for him as righteousness'" (Galatians 3:6, based on Genesis 15:6, translated by the author. See also Romans 4:3.)

(We need here to recall briefly what "righteousness" means for Paul. Righteousness means a good, full relationship to God. It is not a quality which we have in ourselves, but the quality of our standing with God. For Paul, as for many other Jews, the great goal of human life is to attain righteousness, to find God's good favor.)

Paul shows that Abraham was counted as righteous even though there was no law for him to obey. Then Paul finds the grounds on which Abraham was accounted righteous. He was accounted righteous because he "had *faith* in God."

Paul finds another text which combines the hope for righteousness with the stress on faith. This is Habakkuk 2:4, which Paul quotes in Galatians 3:11 and Romans 1:17. The Greek can be translated in two ways, and Paul apparently thinks that the text means both things:

(1) "The righteous one will live by faith." That is, the righteous person lives in a certain way, namely, faithfully.

(2) "The one who is righteous by faith shall live." That is, the person whose righteousness comes from faith will have life. Even after death, the faithful person will be made eternally right with God.

Paul uses the text on Abraham and the text from Habakkuk to make his point against his Galatian opponents: righteousness does not come from the law. Righteousness comes from faith, and faith is the very opposite of the law.

Though the law for Paul is clearly the Jewish law, the law represents all those ways in which human beings *strive to win* their righteousness—their right relation to God. The law represents all those ways in which human beings try to *achieve* God's approval.

We can translate that picture of the law as human striving for righteousness into terms which make sense for our own situation. Sometimes that striving for righteousness is the effort to achieve God's favor by our *piety.* We turn to prayer, not as a gift, but as a way to win favor. We study the Bible, not as a guide, but as an obligatory homework assignment from an exacting Eternal Teacher. We go to church, not out of the joy of praising God in the company of other Christians, but because we suspect that when the roll is called up yonder, someone will hand out gold attendance pins to the faithful.

Sometimes our striving for righteousness is the effort to achieve God's favor by our *ethical uprightness.* We engage in the causes which seek justice, not out of concern for the oppressed, but because we hope that our attempts will be eternally noticed. Or we refrain from practices we consider immoral, not because of their immorality, but because we suspect that someone is watching, and we don't want to get caught.

Sometimes our striving for righteousness is the effort to achieve

God's favor by the *rightness of our theology*. Instead of rejoicing in what we *can* believe, we worry about what we *must* believe. We compile lists of the essential dogmas of Christian life, and we check ourselves—and our neighbors—to see how well we are doing. We suspect that unless we believe the right propositions and unless we can recite them in the proper language, we shall never have God's favor. Sometimes we claim that this concern with right doctrine is what Paul means when he says we are made righteous by faith, but we shall see that that is not what Paul means at all.

All these ways in which we strive for God's favor are our ways of keeping the law, and they stand radically against Paul's insistence that God's favor is always and only received through faith.

As we have noted,[1] Paul suggests that the attempt to win God's favor by keeping the law leads in one of two directions.

(1) Sometimes it leads to despair. Paul speaks of people under the law and says that too often they find themselves incapable of living up to the standards they set for themselves, unable to win God's favor as they had intended to do:

> . . . . For I do not do what I want, but I do the very thing I hate.
> So I find it to be a law that when I want to do right, evil lies close at hand.
> For I delight in the law of God, in my inmost self, but I see in my members
> another law at war with the law of my mind and making me captive to the
> law of sin which dwells in my members (Romans 7:15, 21-23).

When such people discover that they are not following the law, they feel themselves cut off from God, without hope of any right relationship. This is the despair of which Paul writes:

> Wretched man that I am! Who will deliver me from this body of death?
> (Romans 7:24).

(2) Sometimes the attempt to win God's favor by keeping the law leads to pride, or, in Paul's terms, "boasting." Paul implies that one great danger of living under the law is that people may feel that they have *earned* God's favor by the splendid way in which they have followed the law's commands. This leads to intolerable *self*-righteousness, even before God. This is part of Paul's argument in his letter to the Romans:

> Then what becomes of our boasting? It is excluded. On what principle?
> On the principle of works [i.e., of the law]? No, but on the principle of
> faith (Romans 3:27; cf. also Romans 2:17, 23).

Again, Paul points to Abraham as the example of one who is

saved by his faith from the danger of boasting: "If Abraham was justified by works, he has something to boast about, but not before God" (Romans 4:2).

In another context, Paul sums up his view of boasting: "'Let him who boasts, boast of the Lord.' For it is not the man who commends himself that is accepted, but the man whom the Lord commends" (2 Corinthians 10:17-18).[2]

The trouble with both despair and pride is that they separate us from God. Despair causes a person to say: "I'm so miserable that God can't help me." Pride causes a person to say: "I'm so splendid that God doesn't need to help me." In either case we are driven from God just when we should be driven toward God. Therefore, the law, which was meant to turn us toward God, drives us from God just because it produces despair or pride. That is, the law itself provides the opportunity for sin:

> For no human being will be justified in [God's] sight by works of the law, since through the law comes knowledge of sin (Romans 3:20).

> Is the law then against the promises of God? Certainly not; for if a law had been given which could make alive, then righteousness would indeed be by the law. But the scripture consigned all things to sin, that what was promised to faith in Jesus Christ might be given to those who believe [have faith] (Galatians 3:21-22).

Again, we can see in our own situation how our forms of striving can lead to despair or to pride and therefore separate us from God.

When we try to achieve righteousness by our *piety,* it is easy to fall into despair. We need only measure our achievements against our hopes. Particularly when it comes to prayer, we run the risk of testing our success as spiritual athletes and finding that we fall short. Our failure constantly to know the presence of God becomes a sign for us that we have lost God's favor. We had hoped that in prayer God would come near; we discover that it is just as we pray that God seems far away, and we fall into despair.

It is equally easy to slip into pride in our piety. All those attendance pins and offices and honors we flaunt before God are hallmarks of our pride. Even testimonials on how we were saved— valuable as those may be—run the danger of focusing on *our* salvation rather than on the God who saves us.

Our striving for *ethical uprightness* can also lead to despair. It is not simply that our best intentions are not good enough or that our willpower goes wobbly at the crucial moment. More than that, we easily become so committed to our own vision of justice that when our programs fail, we assume that God has failed. My own generation began with a passionate zeal for peace (as we understood peace) and racial justice (as we imagined racial justice). When neither peace nor justice arrived on our own terms, either we despairingly turned cute and cynical, or we headed for the woods.

Equally, the search for God's favor through moral zeal can lead to pride. Our ethical principles become the absolute standards by which we test other people and even God. A. King Boutwell tells the story of a woman in a church he served who was a fervent teetotaller. At one point in a talk before the women's society, Boutwell made some reference to Jesus' drinking wine. After the talk, the abstemious woman, thoroughly outraged, asked Boutwell if he really believed that Jesus drank alcoholic beverages. Boutwell said that the biblical evidence indicated overwhelmingly that Jesus did drink wine. "Well," said the woman, "if he did that, he's no Lord of mine." .

So, too, many of us who were committed to the "movements" of the sixties judged not only the integrity of our elders but also the faithfulness of God by the standard of our own convictions, .Our certainty of our own rightness too easily turned into a bitter and self-congratulatory distancing, not only from other Christians, but also from the God we thought we had failed. All such pride in our own moral rightness turns us from openness to the God whom we are called to serve in God's own "movement" toward justice in the world.

Our search for *right belief* can lead to despair. When we set up for ourselves a list of dogmas we are supposed to believe and then we fail to believe, we assume that God is as attached to our dogmas as we. We are dissatisfied with ourselves and imagine God's dissatisfaction.

Or the search for right belief can lead to pride. We presume to have discovered God's truth and to hold it fast. We hold it fast against all opposition, even against the constant, sneaky opposition of the One who makes all things new. Clinging to our own version of God's truth, we ignore the true God and fall into sin.

In all these ways, though we do not despair over circumcision or take pride in keeping the sabbath, we still pretend to live under the law.

Christ as the End of the Law

For Paul the law is the mark of the Old Age in human history. It marks the way in which people dealt with God from the time of Moses until the time of Christ, during the era which is now passing away:

> Now before faith came, we were confined under the law, kept under restraint until faith should be revealed. So that the law was our custodian until Christ came, that we might be justified by faith. But now that faith has come, we are no longer under a custodian; for in Christ Jesus you are all sons of God, through faith (Galatians 3:23-26).

The law is also the mark of the Old Age in the life of each believer. Each believer *has* lived with his or her own kind of striving after God's favor. Each believer has therefore fallen into despair or slipped into pride. However, now, through faith, believers become citizens of the New Age. As a sign that they are citizens of the New Age, they receive the gift of the Spirit of God. When they forget that they are citizens of the New Age, when they retreat from faith to the law, then they pretend to be what they are not. They pretend to be citizens of that age which is already passing away.

> O foolish Galatians! Who has bewitched you, before whose eyes Jesus Christ was publicly portrayed as crucified? Let me ask you only this: Did you receive the Spirit by works of the law, or by hearing with faith? Are you so foolish? Having begun with the Spirit, are you now ending with the flesh? Did you experience so many things in vain?—if it really is in vain. Does he who supplies the Spirit to you and works miracles among you do so by works of the law, or by hearing with faith? (Galatians 3:1-5).

Paul, however, knows that the Old Age has been overthrown and is passing away. He knows that the law is no longer valid. He knows this because he knows what God has done in Jesus Christ: "For Christ is the *end of the law,* that every one who has faith may be justified [or made righteous]" (Romans 10:4, author's italics).

Paul explains the way in which Christ ends the Old Age and begins the new in a number of different ways in his epistles. Two of these explanations are especially pertinent when we try to understand the way in which the cross of Christ ends the power of the law in our lives.

(1) The cross as a "curse":

This first explanation is part of a *midrash* in Galatians 3. A midrash is an interpretation of Scripture which often explains one verse of the Old Testament in the light of another verse. These *midrashim* often seem very complicated to us, and Paul's midrash here is no exception; but it can still help us to understand the reasons why Paul believes that Christ is the end of the law.

> For all who rely on works of the law are under a curse; for it is written,

"Cursed be every one who does not abide by all things written in the book of the law, and do them." Now it is evident that no man is justified before God by the law; for "He who through faith is righteous shall live"; but the law does not rest on faith, for "He who does them shall live by them." Christ redeemed us from the curse of the law, having become a curse for us—for it is written, "Cursed be every one who hangs on a tree"—that in Christ Jesus the blessing of Abraham might come upon the Gentiles, that we might receive the promise of the Spirit through faith (Galatians 3:10-14).

We can begin by trying to interpret this as narrowly as we can, and then we shall try to explain the interpretation in terms which may be somewhat easier to understand.

Paul is making an argument based on Scripture. The heart of the argument is that, according to Scripture itself, people who live under the law are bound to obey every command and decree of the law, however minor it may seem. Of course, no one *can* obey every detail of the law; so if our relation to God depended only on obeying the law, we would all be cursed. Wondrously, however, Jesus Christ has taken upon himself that curse which we deserved. Therefore, the age of the law and the age of its curse are over. In the crucifixion Christ has removed us both from the power of the curse and from the power of the law. He has established the New Age, the age of faith.

Perhaps we can translate some of the meaning of Paul's claim into our own terms. First, Paul implies that the law finally proves its own impossibility in the cross of Christ. For to what did the law lead? It led to the crucifixion, outrage, disgrace, and cursing of God's Chosen One. That is, the end result of human striving after God's goodness was that when God's goodness appeared in the flesh, we crucified Christ as an outlaw.

That idea is not so foreign to us as it may seem. When we strive to win God's goodness by our piety, we are offended by the ways in which God sometimes works in impious, unexpected, and disgraceful ways. We tend to curse those irreligious people who may yet be the revealers of God's love.

When we strive to win God's favor by doing good, we are offended by any indication that God extends God's favor to those who are not as good as we. We tend to curse that injustice by which those who do not agree with our view of God's cause sometimes triumph and often prosper. In that way we curse the very providence of God.

When we strive to win God's favor by believing the right things, we are offended when God does good through heretics and unbelievers. We are concerned when they lead grace-filled lives without even knowing the meaning of the word "grace." We therefore curse the unfairness of God who seems to accept their falsehood and ignore our truth.

The result of our striving after God's favor is our inability to accept God's favor apart from our striving. It is our inability to believe in God on God's terms rather than our own. Therefore, we do curse God and those whom God chooses to reveal God's favor.

A second translation of Paul's claim is this. Paul suggests that all of us know our own inability to fulfill the requirements of the law. That is, when we are honest, we know that we fail in our striving to be good enough to win God's favor. We know that we do not deserve God's love, and, therefore, we convince ourselves that we do not have God's love. All that is turned around in the cross of Christ. In the cross God's Chosen One took on the sense of judgment which he did not deserve. We receive the mercy we could not imagine. Therefore, the tables are turned on our sense of judgment. God does not deal with us according to our understanding of merits and demerits. God deals with us according to God's free pleasure. Happily, that means that God deals with us according to God's great love.

(2) The cross as a gift:

Paul explains Christ's bringing of the New Age in another way which is especially pertinent to our understanding of faith. For Paul, Christ ends the age of the law because in Christ God's love is sheer gift. Under the law we strove to win God's love. In the cross we see that we can't win God's love and that we don't need to win God's love because God's love is there for us as a gift:

> While we were still weak [that is, when our striving could win us nothing], . . . Christ died for the ungodly [that is, for those who did not or could not keep the law]. Why, one will hardly die for a righteous man— though perhaps for a good man one will dare even to die. But God shows his love for us in that while we were yet sinners Christ died for us (Romans 5:6-8).

> For the wages of sin is death, but the *free gift* of God is eternal life in Christ Jesus our Lord (Romans 6:23, author's italics).

The cross as the free gift of God's love stands over the despair which striving after the law produces. We no longer need to earn God's love by anything we do; so we need not feel shame or guilt when we fail to earn God's love. We realize that a right relationship to God does not depend on our achievements but on God's mercy. We realize that that mercy is given us in the cross of Christ. Therefore, we no longer despair.

The cross as the free gift of God's love stands over the pride which striving after the law produces. We discover that we no longer *can* earn God's love by anything we do. We discover that God's love is available only as a free gift. There is no way that we can earn it and therefore no way in which we can boast about earning it.

For Paul the cross of Christ is the great dividing line between the Old Age of the law and the New Age of faith. The cross destroys the law and its striving because it provides what the law could never provide. It provides a right relationship to God. It provides that right relationship on the only possible terms: not as something we win from God, but as something God does *for* us. God does love us absolutely. Nothing we can do will win that love, but nothing we can do will end that love either.[3]

Faith Instead of Law

Since we cannot earn God's love and need not earn God's love, what can we do? What need we do? We can and need to *receive* God's love. We can receive the free gift. And for Paul the way in which we receive that gift is by faith.

More accurately, what Paul means by "faith" is receiving the gift of God's love. When we have faith, we acknowledge that God does work out God's love in the cross of Christ. When we have faith, we acknowledge that the word of God's love is a word about ourselves.

Paul says that we receive that love, that we are faithful, through *hearing:*

> O foolish Galatians! Who has bewitched you, before whose eyes . . . Christ was publicly portrayed as crucified? Let me ask you only this: Did you receive the Spirit by works of the law, or by hearing with faith? (Galatians 3:1-2).

For Paul, the Galatians were foolish because they refused to acknowledge what was before their very eyes—Christ on the cross. The fact of Christ on the cross should have made plain to them that God's love was given them as a completely free gift. All they were asked to do was *hear* the word of God's love. All they were asked to do was receive God's love. That hearing, that receiving, is faith.

In Romans, Paul ties the need to hear through faith explicitly to the church's ministry of proclamation:

> But how are men to call upon him in whom they have not had faith? And how are they to have faith in him of whom they have never heard? And how are they to hear without a preacher? . . . But they have not all heeded the gospel; for Isaiah says, "Lord, who has had faith in what he has heard from us?" So faith comes from what is heard, and what is heard comes by the preaching of Christ (Romans 10:14-17, emended by the author).

We see here how consistently the picture of faith is tied to the business of preaching and hearing. To have faith is to hear the word of the cross as it is proclaimed and to accept it as the true word of God's love.

In movies about ocean travel, when the captain has an announcement of crucial importance, he calls over the loudspeaker: "Now hear this!" Passengers are supposed to pay strict attention, knowing that the word they will hear is a word of utmost importance and a word which directly affects their own lives. Paul says that the gospel addresses people with God's "Now hear this!" Faith is paying strict attention to that word, knowing that that word is of utmost importance and acknowledging that that word is a word about us.

The fact that faith is, first of all, a matter of hearing has two implications for Paul's theology.

First, it implies that there is a place in the Christian life for a kind of hopeful passivity. The problem with Paul's Galatian opponents and with some of the Jews he writes about in Romans is that they are so busy *doing* things to win God's favor that they haven't learned to sit still long enough to hear the word that God's favor is a free gift. That is why Paul contrasts "works of the law" with "hearing with faith" in Galatians 3:2. Paul here suggests what the story of Mary and Martha in Luke's Gospel suggests. (Cf. Luke 10:38-42.) It is not that Martha does anything positively wrong by running about being "distracted with much serving." The problem is that she has not learned the art of passivity. She does not realize that there is a time to receive, to sit still, to accept the love and mercy of God in Jesus Christ. Mary sits there and hears with faith. That is why she has "chosen the good portion."

We need hardly note that American churches are especially prone to a kind of frenzied activity. Either we spend enormous amounts of time taking care of our own fellowship—with potlucks, study groups, meetings, and bazaars; or we spend enormous amounts of time trying to serve our community—with service projects, fund-raising drives, meetings, and bazaars. Often we are most ill-at-ease at that time which ought to be the center of our life together: that hour on Sunday when we are to hear, to receive the word of God's love. We feel that that hour is a waste of time because we're not *doing* anything. Our anxiety over passivity is not just a tribute to our American gift for hyperactivity. It is a sign of bad faith. It is a sign of our inability to receive anything as a gift—even the word of God's love in Jesus Christ. (It need hardly be said that passivity isn't the last word concerning faith—see the next chapter—but it is the first word, and the hardest word, for most of us to accept.)

The fact that faith is a matter of hearing has a further implication for Paul. It helps solve that pastoral problem which drove him to his stress on faith in the first place. The pastoral problem was: "What shall we do with Gentiles who become Christian?" The danger was that the church would become an exclusive little band of Jewish Christians or of Jews and Gentiles who were willing to act like Jews.

The great advantage of the claim that our righteousness comes by hearing with faith is that hearing with faith is something everyone can do. Faith, unlike works, has a universal quality. If salvation came through works, it might be restricted to those who did works of special piety—like the Galatians who kept the Jewish law. Or it might be restricted to those who were especially learned or wise—as the Corinthians thought they were. But salvation comes in the very simplest of ways. It comes through hearing the word of God's love and accepting that word. Because faith comes in so simple a way, faith is available to everyone: Jews and Gentiles, wise and foolish alike:

> But now the righteousness of God has been manifested apart from law [and apart from wisdom, too, we might add], although the law and the prophets bear witness to it, the righteousness of God *through faith in Jesus Christ for all who* [*have faith*]. For there is no distinction; since all have sinned and fall short of the glory of God, [all] are justified by his grace as a gift, through the redemption which is in Christ Jesus (Romans 3:21-24, author's italics and emendations).

In Galatians Paul makes a similar point:

> But now that faith has come, we are no longer under a custodian; for in Christ Jesus *you are all* sons of God, *through faith.* For as many of you as were baptized into Christ have put on Christ. There is neither Jew nor Greek, there is neither slave nor free, there is neither male nor female; for *you are all one* in Christ Jesus (Galatians 3:25-28, author's italics).

Again, we can only confess that our churches, like Paul's churches, run the danger of holding an exclusivistic, and therefore a false, understanding of faith. Evangelicals assume that people who do not hold a sufficiently literalistic view of biblical interpretation cannot be faithful. But faith, as Paul understands it, is certainly not tied to any one way of interpreting Scripture. It is the way in which we hear the word of God's love, and no doctrine of inspiration can limit that hearing. Liberals assume that people who do not hold a sufficiently sophisticated, "modern" world view cannot be faithful. But faith, as Paul understands it, is not bound by any understanding of the way the world goes—however compelling. Faith is the way in which we accept God's mercy, and no cultural or educational "limitations" need hinder that acceptance.

Those of us whose life-style is basically "straight" often feel that those whose lives are less traditional and less socially acceptable cannot possibly be faithful. But faith, for Paul, is not tied to one way of eating, dressing, shaving, or making music. Faith is hearing the word of God's love as a word for oneself. No life-style need hinder that hearing. Those of us whose life-style is more novel too easily think that straight people cannot possibly be faithful—that they are simply too bound by old ways to receive new promises. But the promise of God is given to all who will receive the promise; neither apparent conformity nor undue formality can prevent the grace of God from declaring itself again and again.

In our churches we might do well to see whether the faith we profess is the faith Paul professes. There is one helpful clue. If we are marked primarily by our exclusiveness; if we all think alike, look alike, and act alike; our faith is probably far too small. If we are rich in our diversity and easy in our acceptance of one another, we may be moving toward a rich understanding of what faith really is.

The fact that hearing by faith suggests both the passivity and the universality of faith relates directly to Paul's view of the church as the community of the New Age.

Because the church is the community without credentials, Christians know that there is nothing they can do to earn a right relationship with God. They know that they can only receive that right relationship as a free gift. That receiving is called faith.

Because the church is the community without distinctions, Christians know that they have no special claim on God's love, no reason to vaunt their worth against that of their brothers and sisters. They know that all are equally addressed with and free to hear the word of God's love. That hearing is called faith.

Faith, therefore, stands against the frantic activity and the narrow exclusiveness of the law. Faith calls us to a passive waiting upon God's word and recalls us to the universality of the gospel. It is the proper mark of that community which lives in the New Age, freed both from the law and from the quest for both credentials and distinctions.

We need now to look more specifically at the shape of that faith to which Paul calls his churches.

The Shape of Faith

Past, Present, and Future

For Paul, faith includes affirmations about the *past*. Everything Paul wants to say about God's love for humankind finds its focus in a particular series of events in the past—the crucifixion and resurrection of Jesus. If God was not active in these past events, then there is no point in talking about the present significance of faith:

> If Christ has not been raised, then our preaching is in vain and your faith is in vain. We are even found to be misrepresenting God, because we testified of God that he raised Christ . . . (1 Corinthians 15:14-15).

In one of his great summaries of his faith, Paul refers to reconciliation not just as a present reality but as something God has done at a specific point in history.

> God *was* in Christ reconciling the world to himself, not counting their trespasses against them . . . (2 Corinthians 5:19, with author's italics and emendations).

So for Paul, faith is not simply a present relationship to God or an openness to God's future. Faith also involves a particular understanding of God's activity in the past.

However, what that understanding of the past makes possible is the affirmation that God is still a loving *presence* in history and in the lives of men and women. Just because Paul believes that God has reconciled the world to God's self in Christ, he can speak in the present tense to his Corinthian readers: "We beseech you [for] Christ, be reconciled to God" (2 Corinthians 5:20*b*). God's gracious activity on our behalf in the cross and resurrection is the clear sign that God continues to deal graciously with us as individuals, with the church, with societies, and with nations. That is why Paul writes: "We know that in everything God is working for the good together with those who love him" (Romans 8:28, emended by the author). The power and mercy of God which were made available in the cross are still available to those who hear the word of the cross and receive it in faith:

> For I decided to know nothing among you except Jesus Christ and him crucified. And I was with you in weakness and in much fear and trembling; and my speech and my message were not in plausible words of wisdom, but in demonstration of the Spirit and of power, that your faith might not rest in the wisdom of men but in the power of God (1 Corinthians 2:2-5).

Faith also looks to the *future*. God who acted in the cross and resurrection of Christ in the past, who is present in human life and in human history, will bring the fullness of the kingdom in the future.

That kingdom will mean eternal life with Christ for the believer, and the faith which looks to the future affirms that personal hope:

> For if we have been united with him in a death like his, we shall certainly be united with him in a resurrection like his. We know that our old self was crucified with him so that the sinful body might be destroyed, and we might no longer be enslaved to sin. For he who has died is freed from sin. But if we have died with Christ, we *have faith* that we shall also live with him (Romans 6:5-8, emended by the author).

The kingdom (which is already beginning) will also mean new life for the whole created order, and faith looks confidently toward a future in which the entire universe is redeemed by God's mercy:

> I consider that the sufferings of this present time are not worth comparing with the glory that is to be revealed to us. For the creation waits with eager longing for the revealing of the sons of God . . . because the creation itself will be set free from its bondage to decay and obtain the glorious liberty of the children of God (Romans 8:18-21).

In writing to the Corinthians, Paul uses other images to express that hope which is part of his faith:

> Then comes the end, when [Christ] delivers the kingdom to God the Father after destroying every rule and every authority and power. For he must reign until he has put all his enemies under his feet. The last enemy to be destroyed is death. . . . When all things are subjected to him, then the Son himself will also be subjected to him who put all things under him, that God may be everything to every one (1 Corinthians 15:24-28).

We have seen that Paul uses Abraham as the great example of a faithful person. One important feature of Abraham's faith is the hope with which Abraham looked to the future. Against all evidence and against all odds, Abraham believed God's word that God would give Abraham a son and through that son a great nation. Abraham becomes a model for Christian people, who are called to hope against sometimes overwhelming evidence to the contrary, that in Jesus Christ God has made us all God's sons and daughters and will finally give to us and to all creation a heritage rich beyond imagining:

> In hope [Abraham] had faith against hope, that he should become the father of many nations; as he had been told, "So shall your descendants be." He did not weaken in faith when he considered his own body, which was as good as dead because he was about a hundred years old, or when he considered the barrenness of Sarah's womb. No distrust made him waver concerning the promise of God, but he grew strong in his faith as he gave glory to God, fully convinced that God was able to do what he had promised (Romans 4:18-21, emended by the author).

Paul's understanding of the past, the present, and the future dimensions of faith corresponds to Paul's understanding of the New Age, the new creation. For Paul that New Age has already begun in the cross of Jesus and in his resurrection. Therefore, people living in the New Age live with a faith which includes the affirmation of those past events when the New Age began. For Paul the New Age is also that present reality in which Christian people live. Therefore, Christians affirm the reality of God's presence in their lives and in the movement of human history. However, for Paul the fullness of the New Age is yet to come. Therefore, Christian faith always contains a strong element of hope as we wait patiently and confidently for that day when God shall be all in all.

Sometimes it is very difficult for us to hold on to the past, the present, and the future dimensions of our faith.

Some of us tend to ignore the past element of faith. We hold the traditional claims about Christ's incarnation, death, and resurrection to be useful stories or helpful myths. Their only real purpose is to help us understand the present and be open to the future. We can know God's love in our own lives and hope for God's love in the time to come without needing to make any claims about what God has done in the past. For Paul, however, the incarnation, cross, and resurrection of Christ are precisely the places where God showed that love; and if those past events have no claim to validity, we have no adequate reason to trust in God's present or future love. More than that, in the cross and resurrection God did not simply show God's love. God acted out God's love. God *did* God's love. God *did* reconcile the world to God's self. If God did not reconcile the world to God's self in the cross and resurrection, then the world is not reconciled to God. Our present faith and our future hope are deluded.

We pretend that we live in the New Age, but there is no New Age unless that New Age broke into human history in Jesus' life and death and resurrection.

Some of us tend to ignore the present element of faith. We think that faith is sufficient if it believes the "sacred facts" about Jesus and hopes for a blessed future with God. God's only present function is apparently to instruct us about what God used to do in the good old days and is apt to do in the glorious future. We are therefore not open to the word of God which is ever rich and new. We are closed to the possibility of present inspiration, divine surprise. We tend to ignore the ways in which God is working out God's kingdom within the kingdoms of this world. We tend to be too suspicious of movements toward greater justice and greater freedom in the present because we deny that God can be in those movements. Therefore, we too easily abdicate responsibility for this present world and this present time, forgetting that our faith is faith in the God who is now "working with us for what is good" (Romans 8:28a, emended by the author).

Some of us are skeptical of the future element of faith. We believe what God has done in the past, and we trust what God is doing in the present. We do not, however, have much hope for the future. We suspect that there is no meaningful way in which we can speak of life beyond death, and we fear that we may all too easily destroy God's creation while God stands helplessly by. Yet, the God who has no power over the future is too small a God for Paul. The God Paul sees revealed in Jesus Christ has promised us that death can never be the final word—neither for us nor for our world. Faith includes the hope that, even in the face of death and desolation, God is God and will prevail.

One of our tasks as the church is to remind ourselves and one another that faith can include our past, our present, and our future. Any faith which ignores past, present, or future is not as full and rich as the faith Paul calls us to affirm.

Faith That, Faith In, Faithfulness To

Another way of understanding the shape of faith, as Paul presents it, is to look at the ways in which Paul actually uses the term "faith." "Faith" has at least three closely related meanings for Paul.

Sometimes Paul writes about *faith that*. Faith for him includes *faith that* God is a faithful and loving God. Faith includes *faith that* God has acted in certain ways among people. Faith includes *faith that*

Jesus Christ was and is God's reconciling One. In this sense, the word "faith" means something very similar to "belief."

One clear example of this understanding of faith is in Romans 10:9: ". . . if you confess with your lips that Jesus is Lord and believe [have faith] in your heart that God raised him from the dead, you will be saved." Here faith is *faith that* God has acted in a special way—by raising Christ from the dead.

In 1 Corinthians 15 Paul reminds the Corinthians of that tradition which he has previously passed on to them:

> . . . that Christ died for our sins in accordance with the scriptures, that he was buried, that he was raised on the third day in accordance with the scriptures, and that he appeared to Cephas . . . [and then on through the list of appearances] (1 Corinthians 15:3-8).

Then he goes on to say: "Whether . . . it was I or [the other apostles], so we preach and so you [have] believed [or had faith]" (1 Corinthians 15:11). Again, faith is *faith that* Christ died and God raised him and *faith that* his death and resurrection have saving significance for our own lives.

So, too, when Paul was comforting the Thessalonians in their distress over the death of some of their members, he appealed to their shared faith:

> But we would not have you ignorant, brethren, concerning those who are asleep, that you may not grieve as others do who have no hope. For since we *have faith that* Jesus died and rose again, even so, through Jesus, God will bring with him those who have fallen asleep (1 Thessalonians 4:13-14, emended by the author).

At other times Paul writes about *faith in*. Because God is faithful to us, our faith always includes *faith in* God. Because God has brought us into right relationship with God's self through Jesus Christ, faith includes *faith in* Christ. In this sense, the word "faith" means something like "trust."

The great example of this kind of *faith in* for Paul is Abraham:

> No distrust [or unfaith] made him waver concerning the promise of God, but he grew strong in his faith as he gave glory to God, fully convinced that God was able to do what he had promised. That is why his faith was "reckoned to him as righteousness" (Romans 4:20-22).

When God promised Abraham that Sarah would bear a son, Abraham was called to trust in God's trustworthiness, or to have faith in God's faithfulness. He became an example to Christians who are also called to have faith in the faithful God. "To one who does not work but trusts [has faith in] him who justifies the ungodly, his faith is reckoned as righteousness" (Romans 4:5).

Faith in Christ Jesus, therefore, is in part faith in God's power to love us even when we have not earned that love. It is trust in Christ as the one through whom God comes near to us, accepts us, and calls us to a new creation. That is the kind of faith of which Paul writes in the great section on justification in Romans 3:21-26:

> But now the righteousness of God has been manifested apart from law, although the law and the prophets bear witness to it, the righteousness of God through faith in Jesus Christ for all who believe. For there is no distinction; since all have sinned and fall short of the glory of God, they are justified by his grace as a gift, through the redemption which is in Christ Jesus, whom God put forward as an expiation by his blood, *to be received by faith.* This was to show God's righteousness, because in his divine forbearance he had passed over former sins; it was to prove at the present time that he himself is righteous and that he makes righteous the one who has faith in Jesus (emended by the author).

This *faith in* Christ, however, is not only trust in that God who brings us into right relationship with God's self through Christ. At some points, for Paul, faith in Christ is a trust in the living Christ. It is an ongoing relationship to that one in whom we have been given redemption. Faith becomes a kind of trusting communion:

> I have been crucified with Christ; it is no longer I who live, but Christ who lives in me; and the life I now live in the flesh *I live by faith* in the Son of God, who loved me and gave himself for me (Galatians 2:20, author's italics).

This picture of faith as a trusting relationship (begun but not yet complete) comes to its fullest expression in what may be Paul's last epistle, the letter to the Philippians:

> But whatever gain I had, I counted as loss for the sake of Christ. Indeed I count everything as loss because of the surpassing worth of knowing Christ Jesus my Lord. For his sake I have suffered the loss of all things, and count them as refuse, in order that I may gain Christ and be found in him, not having a righteousness of my own, based on law, but that which is *through faith in Christ,* the righteousness from God that depends on faith; that I may know him and the power of his resurrection, and may share his sufferings, becoming like him in his death, that if possible I may attain the resurrection from the dead (Philippians 3:7-11, author's italics).

Finally, Paul sometimes writes about *faithfulness to* God, or *faithfulness to* Christ. Faith places the believer in a position of responsibility and obligation to the faithful God. In this sense, "faithfulness" is very much like "obedience."[4]

The relation of faith and obedience is explicit in Romans 1:5: "Through [Christ] we have received grace and apostleship to bring about the obedience of faith for the sake of his name among all the nations."

In Romans 6:15ff. Paul writes of obedience in a context very close to those contexts in which he usually writes about faith. We can suggest, therefore, that the obedience of which he writes here is in part what he means by faithfulness:

> What then? Are we to sin because we are not under [the] law but under grace? By no means! Do you not know that if you yield yourselves to any one as obedient slaves, you are slaves of the one whom you obey, either of sin, which leads to death, or of obedience, which leads to righteousness? But thanks be to God, that you who were once slaves of sin have become obedient from the heart to the standard of teaching to which you were committed, and, having been set free from sin, have become slaves of righteousness (Romans 6:15-18).[5]

Though Paul does not put as much stress on obedience as on belief and trust as aspects of "faith," there is no doubt that obedience is a central condition of the Christian life for him. And at some points, that "obedience" seems to be an aspect of faith itself.

Paul therefore suggests that faith includes "faith that," or "belief"; "faith in," or "trust"; and "faithfulness to," or "obedience."

The church which seeks to teach faith, and to teach faithfully, will be concerned with each of these aspects of faith. Each of these aspects of faith is also directly related to the methods of teaching which we examined in the preceding chapter.

When we teach by means of tradition, we are partly teaching "faith that," or "belief." Our goal is to help people remember those "saving facts" of what God has done, to believe them, and to accept them as facts which have immense significance for their own lives.

When we teach by means of proclamation, we are encouraging "faith in," or "trust." We declare the faithfulness of God in the hope that those who hear will be enticed to be faithful to God in return. We preach God's mercy in Christ in the hope that those who hear will accept that mercy for themselves. We hope that they will trust Christ as the one who brings mercy. More than that, we hope that they will have some sense of what Paul means when he says: ". . . it is no longer I who live, but Christ who lives in me; and the life I now live in the flesh I live by faith in the Son of God, who loved me and gave himself for me" (Galatians 2:20). That kind of relationship is the goal of our proclamation.

When we teach by means of exhortation, we are urging others—and ourselves—to grow in faithfulness to God in Christ. We are seeking to move together toward fuller, richer, more imaginative obedience.

Therefore, our uses of tradition, proclamation, and exhortation are all ways in which we as the teaching church seek to encourage one another in faith.

Implications for the Teaching Church

We can briefly summarize Paul's understanding of faith.

Faith stands in total opposition to law—to striving after God's favor. Faith realizes that God's favor is not something we can earn but something which God has given us in the cross of Jesus Christ.

Faith, therefore, is more a matter of hearing than a matter of doing. This means that faith includes an element of passivity. It also means—since everyone is free to hear the word of God's favor—that faith is a possibility for everyone. It is inclusive and not exclusive.

We can describe the shape of faith in two ways. Faith has a past, a present, and a future dimension (because the New Age has begun, is present, and will be consummated). Faith includes faith that God was in Christ (belief), faith in God and Christ (trust), and faithfulness to God in Christ (obedience).

"Faith," therefore, becomes a central term for Paul's entire understanding of citizenship in the New Age; and when we raise the question of how we teach faith, we raise a central question for our whole teaching ministry. How can we possibly teach that kind of faith, which is not just believing a number of propositions or obeying a list of rules, but living as new citizens of a new creation? We teach that kind of faith with fear and trembling, of course, but not without some important clues from Paul and our own experience.

In Romans 1:17, Paul writes: "In the gospel the righteousness of God is revealed from faith to faith" (author's translation). Many interpreters think "from faith to faith" just means "solely through faith"; but the phrase's similarity to Romans 3:3 ("Does their faithlessness nullify the faithfulness of God?") leads me to believe that the verse means: "In the gospel the righteousness of God is revealed from God's faithfulness to our faith." (The whole account of

Abraham in Romans 4 includes this same combination of God's faithfulness and Abraham's faith, though the story doesn't use the word "faithful" in describing God; cf. especially 4:21.)

Since the right relation to God is revealed from God's faithfulness to our faith, then the starting point for us when we seek to teach faith is to trust in God's faithfulness. The premise on which our task as a teaching church is based is this: God is faithful and can use us to call forth faith in others. There is nothing we can do to guarantee that someone else will come to faith. There is nothing we need to do to guarantee that someone else will come to faith. God has promised to use us according to God's good pleasure and in God's good time.

Since we live and teach under that promise, our teaching can be free from despair. We can stop analyzing our every move to see whether we've done our job well enough (of course, we haven't). We can stop wondering whether God has given up on us (of course, God hasn't).

Since we live and teach under that promise, our teaching can be free from pride. If—by the grace of God—something works, if someone in our fellowship comes to faith or to new fullness of faith, then we can recall that it *is* by the grace of God that something worked. We need not boast of how well *our* church school does its job or how many folk wandered forward after *our* splendid sermon.

That is, since we live and teach under the promise of God's faithfulness, we are free to have faith! We are free to accept the word of God's love and mercy as a word for us—as teachers, ministers, church school superintendents. Until we are free to have faith, we can talk about faith all we want; but what others will see is our anxiety or our boastfulness. God, of course, can use our anxiety and our boastfulness to bring faith in others; but it is best not to tempt the Lord our God.

As we begin to have faith ourselves, Paul's suggestion that God's righteousness is revealed "from faith to faith" takes on still further meaning. For now God can use us as faithful teachers to entice faithful learners. Faith may not exactly be contagious, but it is seductive, and we need not be ashamed of that.

(However, lest we forget, the faith that we live is faith in God and not faith in our faithfulness. That means that what we bring to the teaching ministry is the real us, with all our mixture of faith and doubt. What we affirm is that God can use the real us—with all our mixture of faith and doubt—to entice others to faith.)

In chapter 2 we suggested that the *whole* church teaches as a community. The church which teaches is a community of faith. Every aspect of our common life is lived (or should be lived) in confidence in the faithfulness of God.

The church which teaches faith is a church which is free from the law. Its members do not strive to win God's favor or to remind one another of how remarkably pious, rigorously orthodox, or zealously ethical they are.

The church which is free from the law does not spend undue time striving to prove itself before God or the world. It is wary of advertisements for itself. Is it a warm and friendly congregation? Let its conduct proclaim that and its bulletin be silent. Does it engage in important social action? Let it do so whether the local press is present or not. Is it Bible believing, God-fearing, and born again? Let its life show forth what its PR modestly refuses to announce.

Since the faithful church is a church beyond striving, beyond the law, let not competition thrive within its walls. Let the charts of gold stars come down from the bulletin boards. Let the little badges and attendance pins be placed in the offering plate as a sign of our fealty to God. Let the letters of commendation from the denomination on being among the top thirty-two hundred churches in giving be quietly placed on a back shelf. And perhaps (come the kingdom) let some of the diplomas surreptitiously disappear from the pastor's wall.

The church which teaches faith has moved beyond the law. It has moved beyond trying to win God's favor. What it does do is proclaim and hear the word of God's favor.

The teaching church, therefore, is a community which understands the passivity of faith. It doesn't end with passivity but it starts there. It discovers to its own astonishment that they who *wait* upon the Lord shall mount up on wings as eagles; they shall run and not be weary; they shall walk and not faint. We can hope for our churches that from time to time we will remember to listen, wait, rejoice in the gifts which we can never earn but which God never fails to give. Part of our ministry of education involves teaching one another how to receive love, grace, hope. This is one reason why worship and proclamation are and need to be at the center of our lives.

The church which teaches faith also understands the inclusiveness of faith. It has really heard the word that it is God in Christ who saves us, not our own orthodoxy, our own social acceptability, or our own income tax bracket. Therefore, we rejoice when we look around us at the community of faith and discover there those with different beliefs, different social status, and different incomes—to say nothing of different races, ages, and life-styles.

Again, our study of the church as the community which teaches faith brings us to a familiar conclusion. Let the church teach faith by being the church—by being a faithful community.

We can also be more concrete about the shape of that faith which the church teaches.

It is a faith which has dimensions of past, present, and future. Because our faith looks to the past, we are not ashamed to "tell the old, old story." Indeed, we shall tell it as often, as vividly, as winsomely as we can. (Choral readings from the King James Version do not count as either vivid or winsome.) We are unashamedly committed to education which is biblical, and we are wary of those who tell us to look everywhere for our insights except to the biblical witness to what God has done.

However, since our faith is faith in the present activity of God, we must not try to bury God's majesty between the covers of sacred Scripture. Our teaching must indicate that God is active in human history, in the history of our own congregation, and in the lives of its members. We must encourage those we teach to be on the lookout for God—assuming that God not only has something to say *to* our lives but God also has something to say *in* our lives. (We must not think that we have captured the faith if we know what Moses had on those tablets and what Jesus said to his disciples—unless we know what God is saying, right now, and how that relates to Moses and Jesus and the rest.)

Further, since faith is faith in God's future activity, our education must take seriously the question of responsibility for the future. The God who calls us to faithfulness calls us to be faithful stewards of the present so that those who come after will have something to work with in the future. The "secular" world is beginning to take the future with increasing seriousness as our environmental resources run low. The church is concerned with the future not only because we need to pass on sufficient material resources to our children but also because we need to pass on sufficient spiritual resources to our children. We need to anticipate new issues and problems and to speak faithfully to the world that is emerging. All too often we speak boldly to yesterday's problems.

The church which has faith in God's future does not fall into easy despair. We do not accept the popular, "secular" despair which says either that we'll run out of goods before we bomb each other into eternity or vice versa. We accept both God's purpose and our obligation for the future. We will certainly not fall into that quasi-Christian despair which thinks that everything is so evil that God will simply zap the world and do us all in. Keeping ever before us the comforting word of John 3:16 that God so *loved* the world, we must joyfully seek to imitate our Maker and fall in love with the world as well.

I have here no explicit guides for planners of curricula or designers of goals for the church's teaching ministry. But I do have some implicit criteria. Let us hold fast to the biblical Word which is the starting point for our self-understanding and our understanding of the world and its Creator. Let us, however, not assume that God shuffled off to some distant realm immediately after dictating Revelation 22:21. Let us continue to look for and affirm God in the world where God is. Let us bring the Bible to bear on the world and the world to bear on the Bible. And let us do all this with a deep sense of responsibility for the future and its citizens and with a firm confidence that the future is in the hands of God.

Finally, we suggested that the shape of faith includes faith that, faith in, faithfulness to God in Christ. In other words, faith includes belief, trust, obedience.

Therefore, the teaching church will be concerned with right belief. We will not fall into the prevailing fallacy that it doesn't matter what you believe just as long as you believe something. Or that it doesn't matter what you believe just as long as you vote in the right way. Or that it doesn't matter what you believe just as long as you feel warmly toward everyone (in some cases, just as long as you feel everyone warmly). It *does* matter what you believe because it does matter what God has done, and the attempt to believe rightly is the attempt to discern rightly what God has done. We hear a good deal of criticism of professional theology and of "head tripping" in our churches (and even in our seminaries). But if the church soon suffocates from overintellectualism, many of us will be greatly surprised. If we take God seriously enough to be Christians, we take God seriously enough to think carefully about God and to try to arrive at more adequate, compelling, persuasive beliefs.

OF COURSE that doesn't mean that our beliefs save us. God

saves us. And it doesn't mean that we use theology as a means of hitting each other over the head or dividing into opposing armies in the great battles of the faith. Theology is one means by which we *grow together* to a fuller understanding of the mercy of God. The proper mode of theology is conversation rather than competition.

All this is to say that in part the teaching church will *teach* in the fairly traditional way of acquainting its members with the doctrines of the church and helping them think about those doctrines carefully, wisely, openly—perhaps even joyfully.

The teaching church will be concerned with trust—trust toward God, trust toward Jesus Christ. Those who are in the teaching church will seek both to be more trusting and more trustworthy. Trusting can probably never be taught save by experience. The teaching church will be a community where we try to grow in trust toward God. It will also be a community where we try to grow in trust toward one another. Our lives with one another become a kind of parable of our lives with God. As we grow in trust toward one another, we portray the possibility of trust in God. We make it more appealing and more accessible.

The church which teaches trust will hope, pray, and perhaps embody for its members what is traditionally called "the saving knowledge of Jesus Christ." That does not mean the saving knowledge *about* Jesus Christ. There are as many ways of expressing what that knowledge does mean as there are theologies. It means, at the very least, that the teaching church opens people to trust in the Christ who lives. It means that our intent is that all of us may know him as a goad and a comfort, the object of our deepest honor, the goal of our richest hopes.

The teaching church will be concerned with obedience. God's love is a free gift. If we have not said that, we have not said anything. Yet gifts freely given and freely received establish relationships. Relationships change our lives in many ways. For one thing, they change our obligations. When we receive the free gift of God's love in Jesus Christ, we enter a new relationship with God and with Christ. That relationship includes obligation and obedience. The church which teaches faith also teaches faithfulness. Faith does not let us off the hook of responsibility toward God and to one another. The specific shape which that responsibility takes is the shape of love, and love is the subject of our final chapter.

Questions for Discussion

1. What did Paul think was the relationship of faith to the Jewish law? What implications does this have for our understanding of faith?

2. Where do we see the dangers of despair or pride in our own Christian life?

3. What is the relationship of faith to *hearing* for Paul? For us?

4. How is our faith related to the past, to the present, to the future?

5. How can we *teach* faith in our church?

5

What Does the Church Teach? 2. Love

Faith and Love

For Paul, faith and love are the two great realities which mark the New Age. Furthermore, faith and love are integrally related to one another.

Faith and love are related to one another, first, because they are both gifts. As we have seen, faith is not an achievement, something we can strive after. Faith is receiving the word—God's love. It is accepting a gift.

So, too, for Paul, love is not so much an achievement as a gift. When Paul writes to the Corinthians about the spiritual gifts, he insists that there is a variety of different gifts within the church. However, three great gifts are given in common to all Christian people—faith, hope, and love (1 Corinthians 13:13).

When Paul writes to the Galatians, he tries to persuade them to give up the striving which he associates with the law and to accept the gift of God's Spirit. When they receive the gift of God's Spirit, they will also receive the fruit of the Spirit:

> But the fruit of the Spirit is love, joy, peace, patience, kindness, goodness, faith, gentleness, self-control. The law is nothing against these (Galatians 5:22-23, emended by the author).

What Paul here indicates is this. If we *strive* to be loving, we simply fall under the law again. If we set up a list of rules on how to love and set out to obey those rules, then the old problems beset us.

Either we fail to be as loving as we are supposed to be, and we fall into despair; or we think we succeed at being as loving as we are supposed to be, and we slip into pride. In either case, the very attempt to love makes love impossible. Desperate people are too wrapped up in their own misery to turn to others in love. Proud people are too engrossed with their own achievements to turn to others in love. The very attempt to *achieve* love makes love impossible.

Therefore, for Paul, love can only be a gift. It is a gift given by the Spirit of God. It is not something to be won but something to be received, with immense gratitude and joy.

Faith and love are related to one another, second, because love is a result of faith, or faith is a requirement for love. That is why Paul says in Galatians 5:6:

> For in Christ Jesus neither circumcision nor uncircumcision [avails anything], but faith working through love.

We also remember the earlier passage in Galatians about hearing with faith:

> O foolish Galatians! Who has bewitched you, before whose eyes Jesus Christ was publicly portrayed as crucified? Let me ask you only this: Did you receive the Spirit by works of the law, or by hearing with faith? . . . Does he who supplies the Spirit to you and works miracles among you do so by works of the law, or by hearing with faith? (Galatians 3:1-5).

Then, as we have just seen, Paul talks of the fruit of the Spirit; and among the fruit of the Spirit is love. Therefore, the Spirit is received through faith; and because the Spirit is received through faith, love is possible.

In writing to the Thessalonians, Paul closely associates faith with love in his moral exhortation: "But, since we belong to the day, let us be sober, and put on the breastplate of faith and love . . ." (1 Thessalonians 5:8). And in writing to Philemon, Paul says: "I thank my God always when I remember you in my prayers, because I hear of your love and of the faith which you have toward the Lord Jesus and all the saints" (Philemon, vv. 4-5).

The reason that Paul claims that faith works through love is that faith *frees us to love*. For Paul, faith is hearing the word that God loves us. Faith is accepting the Good News that in Jesus Christ God establishes a right relationship with us. When we really hear and accept that word, we are free to love, free to turn to one another.

When we hear the word of God's love for us, we are freed from striving. We no longer need to try to achieve God's love because God's love is given us in the cross of Christ. Therefore, we are free from our anxious attempts to make points with God. Because we are free from that anxiety, we can turn from ourselves and our accomplishments to others and their need. That is the beginning of love.

When we hear the word of God's love for us, we are freed from despair. We no longer need to believe that when we do not live up to our own goals, we have somehow forfeited the love of God. Therefore, we don't need to spend all our time beating our breasts and feeling sorry for ourselves. We know that God loves us, failures though we be, and we can turn to others in caring. That is the beginning of love.

When we hear the word of God's love for us in the cross of Christ, we are freed from pride. We no longer need to defend our own goodness as a means of earning divine favor. Divine favor has been given us apart from any goodness of our own. Therefore, instead of looking eagerly for the proof of our own goodness, we are free to recognize and delight in the goodness of other people. That delight is the beginning of love.

In this way, love is not a command. The gospel's strong word is not, "You must love!" The gospel's strong word is, "You can love!" In the cross of Christ we are freed from having to strive for God's love. In the cross of Christ we are freed from despair at our failure or pride in our success. Striving, despair, and pride are all forms of self-centeredness. In the cross of Christ we are freed from self-centeredness and freed to turn to others.

Faith is therefore related to love in this way: through faith we hear and accept the word of God's love for us; when we hear and accept that word, we are free to love other people.

I have some friends who once cared for a foster son for some years. The young boy entered that family with more than his share of doubts and insecurities. He wanted with all his heart to *prove* his worth, and that turned out to be just the problem.

He strove constantly and loudly to show that he was just as good as any other member of the family, and in his striving he simply alienated himself from the others. Sometimes he felt with bleak despair that he wasn't good enough for anyone to love him. Sometimes he boasted that he was so self-sufficient that no one needed to love him.

The more he strove, despaired, or boasted, the less lovable and the less loving he became. But there was no way he could be argued or coerced into love. All the foster parents could do was to seek to love him as fully, as unconditionally as they could. There was no Hollywood ending to this story; but as this boy began to receive love, he began to give love. As he realized that he didn't need to strive for love, he was freed (somewhat) from his self-centeredness. The despair diminished; the boasting somewhat abated. His love for others was no more perfect than any other human love, but it was increasingly strong and rich.

The story of the boy is a parable of the Christian's life with God. God does not simply stand over us proclaiming: "You must love!" God makes love possible by loving us in the cross of Jesus Christ. When we accept God's love by faith, then we are free to love one another.

Again, this provides a clue for the church's self-understanding today. If our proclamation and our exhortation consist largely of commands—even commands concerning love—we miss the heart of Paul's gospel.

My guess is that most of us church members know perfectly well that we are supposed to love other people and wish desperately that we could. Love will be possible, not as we memorize another set of Scripture verses or try to apply six snappy rules for the loving life. Love will be possible as faith increases. Love will be possible as we hear and accept the word that we are loved. That word will free us from our vast concern with ourselves and will open us to others. In that gift of faith our love begins.

There is a corollary to Paul's understanding of the relationship of faith and love. We Protestants, at least, have continually affirmed that we are justified by faith alone. In Galatians 5:6 Paul tells us how we may guess whether our churches live by faith. Our churches are living by faith if they are also living in love.

If we think that we live by faith, but are spending much of our time bickering with each other on issues of dogma, and if that bickering becomes nasty and unkind, then we can be sure that we're not really living by faith. For faith which is really faith accepts the love of God so confidently that we don't need to bolster our sense of

God's love either by denying that love to those who don't share our theological presuppositions or by trying to force them to conform to our own view.

If we think we live by faith, but are deeply concerned that our church be reserved for people who share our social, ethical, or economic standards, then we can be sure that we're not really living by faith. For faith which is really faith knows that no one *deserves* God's love; all have *received* God's love. Therefore, we can turn, lovingly, to all those other strange people who, like us, have received love they do not deserve.

Paul is very straight on this. If the Galatians do all the things they think are faithful, but don't turn lovingly to one another, their faith is fake faith. They can obey as many rules for right conduct as they choose; but if they don't accept one another (circumcised or not), they're not really faithful (cf. Galatians 5).

If the Corinthians have enough theological skills to fill a major seminary faculty, but turn from one another in selfishness and pride, they are not really living by faith. Unless real love is there among them, real faith is nowhere in sight (cf. 1 Corinthians 13).

Finally, faith and love are not two separate realities for Paul. They are two sides of the same great reality. The starting point for faith and love is God's free gift of love in Jesus Christ. In faith we accept that gift and turn to God with gratitude; in love we accept that gift and turn to others in compassionate service. Where there is no faithful acceptance, there is no compassionate service; but where there is no compassionate service, the faith is only bogus faith.

Love and the Law

Paul has two ways of expressing the relationship of love to the law.

In one sense, love stands against the law. In Galatians 5, the Old Age is strikingly contrasted to the New Age. The Old Age is the age of the law—people strove to win God's favor. It is the age of the flesh. "Flesh" for Paul is the term for all the ways in which people seek to assert themselves, all the ways in which people are self-centered. The New Age, as we have seen, is the age of the Spirit. We can see how closely "flesh" and "law" are related in Paul and how they are contrasted to the Spirit.

But I say, walk by the Spirit, and do not gratify the desires of the flesh. For the desires of the flesh are against the Spirit, and the desires of the

Spirit are against the flesh; for these are opposed to each other, to prevent you from doing what you would. But if you are led by the Spirit you are not under the law (Galatians 5:16-18).

Paul goes on to list the *works* of the flesh. The age of the law, or the age of the flesh, is the age of works; it is the age in which we try to do things to prove our worth. When we try to do things to prove our worth, we become hopelessly self-centered and ignore or abuse other people. So when Paul lists these "works" of the flesh, he includes "enmity, strife, jealousy, anger, selfishness, dissension, party spirit, envy . . ." (Galatians 5:20-21). When we try to work our own goodness, we invariably fall into these disastrously "fleshly," or "selfish," works.

The Spirit, however, is never the result of our striving; it is the gift of God's love received through faith. Those who receive the Spirit have moved outside the realm of the law. Rather than seeking God's favor, they accept the gift of God's favor and are free to turn to one another in love. That is why Paul writes: "The fruit of the Spirit is love, joy, peace, patience, kindness, goodness, faith, gentleness, self-control; against these the law is nothing" (Galatians 5:22-23, emended by the author). The law produces selfishness; the Spirit produces selflessness. The two are literally worlds apart.

In this context, Galatians 5:14 can perhaps best be translated: "For the whole law is wrapped up in the one word, in the 'You shall love your neighbor as yourself'" (author's translation). That is, the whole law is summarized, but more than that, the whole time of law is finished with the one word, "You shall love your neighbor as yourself." That kind of love at once completes and replaces the law.

This same sense that the law is abolished in the new reality of the age of love is also evident in the verse we have already quoted, Galatians 5:6. For Paul, circumcision is the most obvious holdover from the age of the law; and to the Galatians he writes: "For in Christ Jesus neither circumcision nor uncircumcision is of any avail, but faith working through love."

There is, however, another way in which Paul sometimes understands the law. Rightly understood, law is not a way of attaining God's favor. Rightly understood, law can be a way of responding to God's favor. The mistake many of Paul's opponents make in understanding the law is that they think that if people obey it scrupulously, they will have a right relation to God.

Paul insists, however, that God has established that relationship apart from human virtue or deeds. However, precisely because God *has* established a relationship with people, we have obligations under that relationship. Any relationship includes demands of those involved. And that relationship we have to God in Jesus Christ is no exception.

For Paul the New Age has its own set of responsibilities, if you will, its own "law." But it is only because we have received the Spirit of God's love, only because we are already citizens of that New Age, that we can receive and accept the obligations of the new law.

> There is therefore now no condemnation for those who are in Christ Jesus. For the law of the Spirit of life in Christ Jesus has set me free from the law of sin and death. For God has done what the law, weakened by the flesh, could not do: sending his own Son in the likeness of sinful flesh and for sin, he condemned sin in the flesh, in order that the just requirement of the law might be fulfilled in us, who walk not according to the flesh but according to the Spirit (Romans 8:1-4).

And this new law is not unrelated to the Old Testament law. Like Jesus, Paul finds in the command to love the neighbor the summing up of the main ethical insights of the Old Testament (though even here, there is a little of the ambiguity about the law that we saw in Galatians).

> Owe no one anything, except to love one another; for he who loves his neighbor has fulfilled [or "wrapped up"] the law. The commandments, "You shall not commit adultery, You shall not kill, You shall not steal, You shall not covet," and any other commandment, are summed up in this sentence, "You shall love your neighbor as yourself." Love does no wrong to a neighbor; therefore love is the fulfilling of the law (Romans 13:8-10).

Though there is no specific reference to the law in 1 Thessalonians 4, there is the similar suggestion that love for one another is an obligation asked of us by God in response to God's gracious favor:

> But concerning love of the brethren you have no need to have any one write to you, for you yourselves have been taught by God to love one another (1 Thessalonians 4:9).

Paul's claims about the relationship of love to the law guard against two misunderstandings of love.

On the one hand, Paul does not want the concern for love to become part of the strategy of the Old Age, where we tried to gain God's favor by our own achievement. When love becomes that kind of law, all the predictable problems follow. We strive so anxiously to be loving that we find ourselves incapable of love. We turn in on ourselves in despair, thinking that we cannot love. Or we turn to ourselves in pride, thinking that we love so well that our love requires no growing and no sharing. In any of these cases, love becomes impossible, precisely because we have confused love with law.

On the other hand, Paul denies absolutely any claim that the New Age is an age without obligations—toward God or toward the neighbor. Because we are free from the law, we can turn to others in love. Because God has given us God's love in the cross of Christ, we want to respond gratefully, faithfully. That means that we want to turn to others in love. Through Jesus Christ we are brought into a new relationship to God with all the obligations any new relationship imposes. The main obligation this new relationship imposes is the obligation of love.

Two Pictures of Love

Because love is a gift more than a work, Paul cannot simply compile a set of clear rules for being loving. Because love is more of the Spirit than of the law, Paul cannot even say: "This is what you must always do." What Paul can and does do is to draw some pictures of what love looks like—always in regard to some specific situation in the churches to which he writes.

1 Corinthians 13

We have already written of the situation in the Corinthian church at the time of First Corinthians.[1] The church was full of boastful little cliques: some boasted because they preached well, some because they had lots of faith, some (apparently especially loudly) because they could speak in tongues.

Paul drew a picture of love for the Corinthians. He doesn't say: "You must be patient; you must be kind." He says: "Love *is* patient and kind." He describes the gift of love rather than laying down the rules for love. In this way he suggests again that love belongs in an age beyond the law.

Paul's picture of love has three main sections. He first affirms the *worth* of love:

> If I speak in the tongues of men and of angels, but have not love, I am a noisy gong or a clanging cymbal. And if I have prophetic powers, and understand all mysteries and all knowledge, and if I have all faith, so as to remove mountains, but have not love, I am nothing. If I give away all I

have, and if I deliver my body to be burned, but have not love, I gain nothing (1 Corinthians 13:1-3).

The lesser gifts of which Paul writes are those gifts which were especially cherished by the Corinthian church. Some of them valued speaking in tongues, some prophecy, some "wisdom" and knowledge. Some presumably were proud of their faith and some of their sacrifice.

The context of this chapter in First Corinthians suggests why Paul thinks that each of these gifts is worthless without love. When these gifts are exercised without love, they tend to divide the community. They wound the body of Christ. Prophets boast of their prophecy; speakers-in-tongues are proud of their speaking. Each group thinks that it is more "spiritual" than the other. The church begins to fall apart.

The reason that love is necessary to augment the other gifts is that love brings the church together. When love *is* present, then all the other gifts—tongues, prophecy, wisdom—are used in the service of the entire church and not just to build up the egos of those with this gift or that.

Strikingly, for Paul, not even those gifts which he thinks are crucially important—faith and sacrifice—are worth anything apart from love. If faith is used as a ground for self-assertion so that I modestly say, "My faith is so great that I can move mountains," then it's worth nothing. Faith is worthwhile only when it is shared in love. Faith which moves toward our common maturing in the love and knowledge of God is a great gift. Faith which is my little private possession is a fake gift because it is not expanded and disciplined by love.

Sacrifice is worthwhile only when it is done in love. Spectacular feats of self-immolation (physical or psychological) are of no worth unless they actually enrich the lives of others. Those who proudly say: "Look how much I've done for you" or "See what I've sacrificed for the church" need to be sure that what is done or sacrificed is really done or sacrificed for the sake of others, out of love. Otherwise, self-sacrifice is only the subtlest kind of self-aggrandizement, when we pretend to lose our lives knowing perfectly well that we shall be commended for having found them.

After affirming the worth of love, Paul describes the *qualities* of love. When we remember the factionalism and boasting in the church at Corinth, the familiar words take on more power:

> Love is patient and kind; love is not jealous or boastful; it is not arrogant
> or rude. Love does not insist on its own way; it is not irritable or resentful;
> it does not rejoice at wrong, but rejoices in the right. Love bears all things,
> believes all things, hopes all things, endures all things (1 Corinthians 13:4-
> 7).

"Love is patient and kind." In the midst of the Corinthians' (and our) typical striving and self-assertion, love is willing to wait for others. In the midst of the Corinthians' (and our) typical assumption that those who do not agree with them are not worth bothering with, love turns to others with courtesy and generous respect.

"Love is not jealous or boastful." Here are the two sides of the Corinthians' factionalism and pride in their spiritual gifts. Either they treat the gifts they have received as achievements, and boast; or they envy the gifts their fellow Christians have received, and are jealous. Love knows how to receive a gift, as a gift, without boasting. Love knows how to rejoice in the fact that another has other gifts. Love therefore builds up the body of Christ, with its diversity of gifts, all given by the same Spirit.

"Love is not arrogant or rude." Some Corinthians are separated from their fellow Christians by their arrogant assumption that they have a corner on the truth—a corner on wisdom. Love recognizes the false certainty of their own theological correctness for what it is: bad faith. It is bad faith because it suggests that the Corinthians are saved by their theology and not by God's love. Christian love permits no such arrogance because it relies altogether on God's love for all people—whether they share a particular theology or not.

Some Corinthians were separated from their fellow Christians by their rudeness. The wealthy, secure and thoughtless in their own economic security, brought huge meals and full wineskins to the Lord's Supper. Then they obnoxiously flaunted their wealth by eating their fill and drinking too much in the sight of their poorer brothers and sisters. Such behavior mocks the Lord's Supper, which should be that meal where all come together as Christians, apart from any questions of wealth, status, style of life. Love has either the good sense not to flaunt wealth or the good grace to share it. Love certainly does not make a pig of itself while others go hungry.

"Love does not insist on its own way." The great mark of insecure faith is inadequate love. When the Corinthians were not confident that God loved them absolutely in Jesus Christ, they tried to win God's love by other means—by their beliefs, their wisdom, their pious practices. Of course, that attempt to win God's love by other means never gave them any certainty of God's love. "Do we believe the right things?" they wondered. "Is our wisdom really adequate to explain the nature of God?" "Do our religious practices really show that God loves us?" The Corinthians showed their anxiety about God's love in the usual way. They insisted that everyone else should try to win God's love exactly the way they did. Do they believe in baptism for the dead? Then let all Christians believe in baptism for the dead. Do they think that Paul is a wiser teacher than Peter? Then let those poor followers of Peter accept Paul's theology. Do they speak in tongues? Then let every Christian speak in tongues, or else he or she has clearly not received the Spirit. Insecure faith, therefore, becomes unlove. Unlove insists on its own way: "This is the way I believe; so must you also believe." "This is the way I pray; so must you also pray."

Real faith, however, rests in what God has done for us in Jesus Christ. God has loved us absolutely. Real faith, therefore, need feel no insecurity, no uncertainty of God's love. Real faith need not bolster its insecurity by trying to make other people conform to its particular belief, its particular piety, its particular wisdom. Real faith makes possible real love: "Love does not insist on its own way."

"Love is not irritable or resentful." Again, unlove is unlove because it threatens the unity and common care of the church. When some Corinthians were annoyed by what they regarded as other Corinthians' excesses, they failed to accept one another in love. When some Corinthians resented the gifts, the power, or the prestige of other Corinthians in the church, they failed to accept one another in love.

"Love does not rejoice in wrong, but rejoices in the right." It is so easy for those who think Paul is a greater teacher than Peter to rejoice when they hear that the Petrinists had a falling out over the theology of baptism or over the menu for a Corinthian love feast. It is a delight to those who don't speak in tongues when one of the most notorious tongue-speakers delivers a "spiritual" discourse which no prophet— not even the most discerning—is able to interpret. One Corinthian preacher tries not to smile when another Corinthian preacher bombs out. All that, of course, only serves to tear apart the church which should be growing together. Love does not rejoice in all these wrongs; it rejoices in the right. Paul's people delight when Peter's people flourish. Those who are not members of the Corinthian charismatic fellowship rejoice as it flourishes more and more in their midst, while those who are charismatics rejoice with other Christians who receive other gifts. Those who accept their own worth as a gift of God know that their worth is not in the least augmented by the failures of another. Therefore, they take no pleasure in another's failure; but in another's gain they take loving delight.

"Love can take anything. It has complete faith and hope, and it can endure anything" (author's translation). Love has complete faith and hope. It is because the Corinthians were called to complete faith that they could love. It was the faith in God's absolute, unearned love for them which made it possible and necessary for them to turn to others in love. It was their hope that God's love would be the final word for their lives and for human history which allowed them to keep on loving—even when their love for others seemed to be unrewarded or unrequited. They loved because they knew God's love enabled them to love. They continued loving because they hoped that God's love would ultimately triumph. Because love has complete faith, it can take anything. The loving person knows that God's love is not destroyed by anything that other persons or the world can do to one. When we have complete faith, therefore, we are still free to love even when everything seems to go against us. Even when everything seems to go against us, God is still for us. Therefore, we still do not turn to ourselves in self-pity, but we turn to others in love.

Because love has complete hope, it can endure anything. The loving person knows that the pain and unlove which assault one will finally be undone and overcome in the love of God. Therefore, despite pain and unlove, the loving person "hangs in there," enduring all things out of hope in the final mercy of God.

Finally, in this passage Paul affirms the *lasting power* of love:

> Love never ends; as for prophecies, they will pass away; as for tongues, they will cease; as for knowledge, it will pass away. For our knowledge is imperfect and our prophecy is imperfect; but when the perfect comes, the imperfect will pass away. When I was a child, I spoke like a child, I thought like a child, I reasoned like a child; when I became a man, I gave up childish ways. For now we see in a mirror dimly, but then face to face. Now I know in part; then I shall understand fully, even as I have been fully understood. So faith, hope, love abide, these three; but the greatest of these is love (1 Corinthians 13:8-13).

One of the Corinthians' biggest mistakes was that many of them thought that this world was all that there was or was to be. They rightly believed that the New Age had come in Jesus Christ, but they failed to acknowledge that the New Age had not yet come in all its fullness. Perhaps this is one reason why they were so eager to assert their own special worth and their own special gifts. If all that we'll ever see or know of God is what we see or know right now, then perhaps it makes more sense for some of us to insist that we can know more of God by speaking in tongues than by prophesying or vice versa.

Paul, of course, believes that the New Age which has begun in Christ's cross and resurrection is yet to be fulfilled—for the church and for the whole creation (cf. 1 Corinthians 15 and Romans 8). So for Paul, all these gifts which are appropriate for only this side of that fulfillment are of worth, but not of ultimate worth. After all, at the end all of those temporary gifts will pass away.

When God is all things to all people, who will need to speak for God, who will need to prophesy? Who will dare to stand in front of the throne and presume to say what God is up to? What point will there be to having special "spiritual" language when the Spirit is all in all? Why talk about God at all when we are fully in the presence of God? And as for wisdom—wisdom is the way we try to reason about what we can't see very plainly. Wise people are those who stand on one side of a cracked glass and guess what those shadows may be on the other side. But when the glass is taken away, and we see God face to face, there will be no need for wisdom. We won't need to write books about what we can perfectly well see.

All those gifts the Corinthians thought were so important will pass away—who will need them before the throne of God? But love will never pass away. Love will never pass away because when the kingdom comes in all its fullness, we will be together in the presence of God. And that is precisely what love is: love is being *together* in the presence of God. Love is being with one another, and for one another, in the presence of God. None of us will come into that kingdom alone; we will come with our brothers and sisters. And we will know we are in the kingdom, not just because we are with God, but because we are with our brothers and sisters in the fullness of love.

That is why love is the greatest gift—because those little gifts which the Corinthians cherished so much were theirs only for the time between the beginning of the New Age and its consummation. Faith, hope, and love are theirs forever. Faith and hope will be confirmed when God is God altogether and when we see God face to face. Love will be confirmed when the kingdom comes in all its glory; and though faith has become knowledge and hope has become sight, love is still love for all eternity.

It need hardly be added that Paul's insistence that love is the greatest gift continues to apply to our churches today. Whenever our first concern is the lesser gifts—the skill of our preacher, the number of charismatics in our congregation, the size of our Sunday school, the orthodoxy (or modernity) of our beliefs—we tend to move away from each other and away from the unity of the church. Sometimes the division is within a single congregation: liberals arguing with evangelicals or partisans of the choir with partisans of the women's society for a share of the budget.

Sometimes the division is among congregations. We all know the "our-choir-is-better-than-yours" mode of competitive evangelism. And God pity those who try to merge two congregations who believe that the greatest gift God has given each is its remarkably lovely and functional building! Sometimes the division is among larger groups of the body of Christ. Those who think that the greatest gift is their own theological insight tend to separate themselves sharply from the "other camp," however that camp may be defined. And—sadly—those who still believe that the greatest gift God had to give was the Thirty-nine Articles, the Baptist Distinctives, or even the writings of Martin Luther are often eager to mount the battlements whenever threatened by rampant ecumenism or even by any slight hint that we are called into the unity of Christian love.

Since love, however, is the greatest gift, we continue to work and pray for congregations marked more by the love which they share than the separate theologies they espouse or the competing budgets they defend. We continue to work and pray for communities where various congregations work together in that shared ministry which can be a great sign of love among the members of Christ's body. We continue to work and pray for a church universal where—whatever our histories, our polities, or our modes of scriptural interpretation—we can acknowledge one Lord, one faith, one baptism, and one Supper, shared by all of Christ's people, together.

Further, the qualities which Paul ascribes to love are qualities we still seek and encourage in the lives of our churches.

"Love is patient and kind." When each Christian and each group of Christians tends to have a cause to which is ascribed the greatest urgency, it is the gift of love which enables us to wait patiently to understand the causes and agendas of others. In a time when self-assertion and self-assertiveness are the common coins of our realm, the church can be a place where kindness still flourishes.

"Love is not jealous or boastful." It is still as easy for us as it was for the Corinthians to be jealous of the prestige, power, or talents of other Christians or to be boastful about our own prestige, power, or talents. We still seek to be that community in which we acknowledge our worth as the free gift of God so that we need neither boast of our own gifts nor envy the gifts of others.

"Love is not arrogant or rude." We are still prone to theological arrogance, to the appalling certainty that the kingdom has room only for those of our theological stripe. We are still prone to rudeness, even to the rudeness of wealth. American Christians don't often bring rich meals and full wineskins to the table of our Lord while other American Christians suffer. But we American Christians do go home from the Lord's Supper to our Sunday dinners where we consume conspicuously more than the poor of our nation or of other nations would ever dream. That is a rudeness which even the most insensitive Corinthians could not have dreamed.

"Love does not insist on its own way." We still insist on our own way, in each church and among the churches. We confuse our way with the Way and wear little buttons saying One Way, which never means God's way but always means our version of God's way. We hit each other over the head with our versions of God's way. We are astonished that other people aren't bright enough to understand that we are privy to God's little secrets. In so doing, we show bad faith and poor love. We show bad faith by showing that we're so insecure that we need everyone else to agree with us. We show poor love because we don't let others receive God's love in their own way. Love does not insist on its own way. Whenever love sneaks into our churches or our denominations, there is a blessed decline in self-certainty.

"Love is not irritable or resentful." In the pecking order of our churches we tend to be caught between irritation and resentment. We resent those who are higher than we and ignore us. We are irritated by those who are lower than we and annoy us. Love is love because it refuses to admit pecking orders. There are different gifts, but not different ranks, in the kingdom. Therefore, we can be open to others, even to their apparent indifference or (by the mercy of God) to their incessant nagging.

"Love does not rejoice in wrong, but rejoices in the right." Evangelicals and liberals don't compare statistics of church growth in order to delight in the other's failures. We are not overjoyed when a fellow Christian we never much liked gets shown up as a hypocrite or when our theological enemies' prophecies resoundingly fail. When love abounds among us, so does our delight in any growth or mercy given to any member of the body of Christ.

"Love can take anything. It has complete faith and hope, and it can endure anything." Because love is completely hopeful and faithful, the church and our churches do not grow discouraged, even when the prospect for love as a power in this world seems very dim indeed. We trust in the God who is the God of love; and therefore, we do not lose heart when love seems to be ignored in our communities and even in our congregations. Love endures all things.

We hope and seek and pray to grow in love, just as Paul urged the Corinthians to do, because we know that when all is said and done, love is the mark of who we are. The other gifts we think are so important—those buildings, those sermons, those curricula, those anthems—will pass away, and faith and hope and love will endure. But the greatest of these is love, because if there is no love, we can be sure that our faith is fake and our hope is slight. When faith and hope are real, love is real. Therefore, our churches are and are called to be, above all, communities of love.

Philippians 1:9-11

In Philippians, which is a kind of love letter to his favorite church, Paul draws another picture of love:

> And it is my prayer that your love may abound more and more, with knowledge and all moral discernment, so that you may approve what is excellent, and may be pure and blameless for the day of Christ, filled with the fruits of righteousness, which come through Jesus Christ, to the glory and praise of God (Philippians 1:9-11, emended by the author).

Several features of this picture are noteworthy.

First, Paul shows *his* love and concern for the Philippians in his prayer for them. Indeed most of Paul's letters indicate how important prayer was in his ongoing relationship to his churches. For Paul, love is the way in which we turn from ourselves to others. The richest way in which the Christian can turn to another is by bringing that other before God in prayer.

Second, Paul prays that their love may "abound more and more." The quality of love is not limited or measured. We can be sure that whatever can be calculated, quantified, or hoarded is not love.

The more love is given, the more love grows. Just as God's grace for us is never limited but is beyond our imagining, so should our love for one another be beyond measuring. Love is never given because the beloved deserves love; it is always given because the lover wishes to love. Therefore, it can grow more and more.

Third, Paul insists that love include "knowledge" and "moral discernment." Love is not just warm feelings toward the beloved. Love includes knowledge and understanding of the beloved. What does he or she really want? When does the beloved rejoice, so that the lover can share in the joy? When does the beloved hurt, so that the lover can share in the pain? Certainly this is as true a requirement for love in the church as anywhere else.

Love also includes "moral discernment." That is, love is concerned with doing what is right and just, not just what "feels good." The large proportion of his letters which Paul uses for exhortation indicates that he knows that love requires ethical reasoning and moral wisdom. He has little patience with love which simply rushes right in and does what it feels like doing without ever *thinking* ethically about the consequences of its deeds.

Fourth, the love of which Paul writes is love which is "filled with the fruits of righteousness which come through Christ Jesus." This suggests in part what we have already said: love itself is always a gift. It is a gift made possible by the fact that in Jesus Christ we know God's love for us; that is, we are in a right relationship to God. We have received "righteousness." Because we have received righteousness as a free gift, we are free from worry about ourselves and are free to turn to other people in love.

There is another possible implication here. Paul's concern is that the Philippians' love may be "pure and blameless" before God. It may be that he is also saying that "right" love is also a gift of God—that God takes the love we give (which is always growing and needs to grow) and by God's righteousness in Christ Jesus makes that love more "pure" and "blameless" than we could ever have believed. Therefore, God takes our imperfect love and makes it the perfect instrument of God's goodness.

Finally, Paul says that the Philippians' love is a gift which grows "to the glory and praise of God." For Paul, life in the New Age is life which is lived for the glory and praise of God. The faith and the love which are marks of the New Age are marks of the life which is lived to the glory and praise of God. Therefore, Paul suggests, we are called to love, not just because love makes for good human relationships (though that is true), nor just because love enriches our own lives (though that is true), nor even just because love upbuilds the church (though that is preeminently true). We love because loving is one way in which we praise and glorify God, who loves us and frees us to love one another.

This picture of love which Paul draws for the Philippians is also pertinent to our understanding of our own churches.

One way in which our churches grow in love is by growing in prayer for our members and for those outside the church. When we have loving concern for one another, we will want to remember one another in prayer. When we remember one another in prayer, we will want to show that loving concern in other ways as well.

Because love is spontaneous and abundant, our churches need to question the careful, prudential way in which we usually make decisions: how carefully we protect the building and manage the budget, how cautiously we commit our time to the needs of those outside the church (since time is limited). Love is not limited, however, and we need to ask how well our caution conforms to Paul's prayer that love should keep on growing more and more.

Because love includes knowledge and moral discernment, we must be willing to do the hard homework which love requires. Uninformed goodwill is no substitute for careful ethical reasoning, which tries to understand our faith and the world's complicated needs and to relate them one to another.

This need for knowledge and moral discernment is acute within our congregations. Very often, we can't turn lovingly to one another simply because we don't know one another very well and, therefore, cannot recognize or meet one another's needs. Yet love which is anonymous and distant is fake love. Equally often in our conversations—and our sermons—we ignore thinking through those difficult ethical issues which are bound to affect people in our congregation. How carefully have we thought through the issue of abortion? How carefully have we thought through the difficult ethical questions related to the terminally ill? How carefully have we thought through the question of gay people—their rights in society, their place in the church? All of those issues are personal issues for people in our congregations; and if we do not seek moral insight into those issues, we fail in our obligation to be loving.

So, too, as the church deals with the larger issues of society, we need both greater knowledge and clearer ethical reasoning. I remember with some pain what I thought was a good friendship with a young black man when I was in high school. We shared in student government activities together. He visited my home. He even visited my church. Then we lost track of each other.

Some years later, there were massive race riots in Los Angeles where he and I had grown up, and I read a long interview with my onetime friend in a national news magazine. Only then, years later, did I begin to understand the terrible pain and injustice my black friend had suffered in all those years I thought I knew him. I hadn't even known that the place where he lived (and where I had visited) was called Watts.

When we were friends, I would have said that of course I had Christian love for this young black man (though high school boys are not apt to use the word "love"). However, I neither knew him nor had any "moral insight" into his situation as a black person in America. Love which does not care enough to know the beloved, love which has no ethical insight into another's pain and injustice, is a cheap substitute for the real thing.

It is not enough for our churches to send money to starving people or to support funds for educating minority people (though both, of course, are good and necessary). We need to *understand* as best we can the causes of poverty and the shape of discrimination. We need to discern and argue for those moral principles which guide us in dealing with these issues. We need to work toward those difficult changes which may provide for greater economic and racial justice in this nation and the world. Love which doesn't do that is not love; it is some sentimental imitation of love.

So, too, as we seek to be loving persons and loving churches, we acknowledge that love is nothing we can do but is a gift made possible by God's love in Christ. We also love fearlessly, not because our love is ever perfect, but because we trust in God to take our imperfect love and use it to do God's perfect will.

Like the Philippians, we do all this to God's praise and glory. We know that our lives are lived from God, through God, and to God. When we seek to praise and glorify that God in whom our lives are lived, we turn to one another in love. As we grow in love, as we become more and more the community of love, we more and more faithfully serve one another, and we more and more faithfully praise God.

The Church as the Community of Love

As we have already implied, Paul's concern for love is particularly concern for the life of the church. One way of understanding Paul's idea of the church is to say that for Paul the church is the community of love.

The church is the community of the New Age; and as a community of love, it demonstrates the marks of the New Age.

The church is a community of love because love recognizes no credentials. God's love accepts and redeems every person—regardless of credentials, apart from the question of *deserving* love. Further, the ability to love is never a credential. The love we share with one another is a gift from God; so we cannot prove our worth before God on the basis of that love. More than that, it is only God's love for us, apart from our credentials, which makes it possible for us to *be* loving. It is when we are freed from proving our credentials before God that we are free to show our love to one another. That is why a community without credentials is a community of love.

The church is a community of love because love recognizes no distinctions. The reason that Paul had to write 1 Corinthians 13 was that the Corinthians delighted in distinctions. Many of his descriptions of love in that chapter are reminders that there is no place in the church for some of us to say to others: "We are better than you."

"Love is not jealous or boastful"; that is, it neither envies another's distinctions nor prides itself in its own.

"Love is not arrogant or rude"; that is, it knows no distinctions which give it the right to hurt or ignore others. There are no special prerogatives in love.

"Love does not insist on its own way" because in a church without distinctions no group is certain that its own way is the only way.

"Love is not irritable or resentful" because it does not make the distinction between those people who are not good enough for us to bother with (who irritate us) and those who are too good to bother with us (whom we resent).

"Love does not rejoice in wrong, but rejoices in the right" because there is finally no distinction between another's wrong and ours, another's blessing and our own. When one Christian or one group of Christians is hurt, we are all hurt. When one prospers, we are all enriched.

Where love reigns, no distinctions can survive. Life in the church, life in the new community, is life under love. Therefore, in the church there are no distinctions.

The church is a community of love because love has no end. That love which the church already celebrates in the New Age which has begun, the church will continue to celebrate when the New Age is fulfilled. The communion of saints is a communion of love. It is love which binds us all together—living and dead—in the presence of God now and for all eternity.

Furthermore, Paul's great insistence that the church is Christ's body is in part the insistence that the church is the community of love.

When Paul writes of the interdependence of church members, one on another, he is really writing of love: "The eye cannot say to the hand, 'I have no need of you,' nor again the head to the feet, 'I have no need of you'" (1 Corinthians 12:21).

When Paul argues that members of Christ's body have no right to boast and no reason for shame or self-pity, he is writing of love (cf. 1 Corinthians 12:14-21).

When Paul writes of the "sympathy" within the body of Christ, he is writing of love. It is love which allows us to share one another's sufferings and one another's joy. It is love which allows us to affirm: "There [should] be no discord in the body, but . . . the members [should] have the same care for one another. If one member suffers, all suffer together; if one member is honored, all rejoice together" (1 Corinthians 12:25-26).

This is to say that our description of the church in chapters 1 and 2 can be summed up by saying that the church is the community of love.

Implications for the Teaching Church

Again, we can only bring out in brief form some of the clues for our teaching ministry which have been implicit in our exposition of Paul.

Since love is a gift and not a command, Paul draws pictures of love rather than giving lists of rules. The church which teaches love must also be wary of trying to reduce love to a list of commandments, however inclusive. We must try, rather, to portray love winsomely and persuasively so that people will find love appealing. We must try to portray love imaginatively so that people will be free to discover what love can look like in their own lives.

Again, we must try to find the way in which love can be portrayed in story, song, drama—not just in propositions or essays on the meaning of love. We must hope that the life of our church will be a parable of love—that our structures, our relationships to one another, our worship, our meetings will show forth that kind of freedom to care which is at the heart of love.

We must, however, remember Paul's strictures to the Philippians, and we must recognize that love requires knowledge and moral reasoning. One way to love is to study (though if loving stops with study groups, we're in trouble). We need to bring our minds as well as our hearts to bear on human need. We need to engage in ethical reflection and discussion to grow in understanding of the way love relates to a radically changing and radically needy world. Love requires that we read the newspaper as well as the Bible, and a good deal of psychology, economics, and political science as well.

As teachers (whatever our "official" role in the church), we must remember that love begets love. We must teach love, not by telling our students that they must love, but by loving them. Only as they discover that they are loved will they be free to be loving. John's first epistle says that "we love, because [God] first loved us" (1 John 4:19). Most of us can say of some member of our family, some teacher, some friend: "We love because he or she first loved us." Much of our teaching will be done by loving.

Of course, we must also teach lovingly. We must be more concerned with those we teach than with *our* instruction, however wise it may be. We must want to listen to them, to respect them, to learn from them. We must not "insist on our own way."

As teachers (as Christians), we must remember that love receives love. There is no question of the reciprocal love Paul had with his churches. He needed them as much as they needed him. There is no distinction in the church between those who give love and those who receive love; all of us do both. We teach love in part by our ability to receive love gratefully and graciously and by our willingness to acknowledge that we need love—altogether.

In teaching love, the church best teaches by being the church. We teach people how to be loving by being loving. Just when we are the community without credentials, distinctions, or end, we enable our people to turn to one another and to the world in love.

Paul's constant reminder to his churches is: "Be what you are!" We shall be an effective teaching church when we are free to be what we are. We shall be an effective teaching church when we can receive the gifts of faith, hope, and love and share those gifts with others.

We shall be the teaching church when our lives show forth what our curricula proclaim: that the greatest of all God's gifts is love.

Questions for Discussion

1. Why does Paul claim that faith and love are integrally related to one another?

2. What does Paul see as the relationship between love and law? How does this understanding affect our teaching concerning the Christian life?

3. Why does Paul think that love is central to the Christian life and to the Christian community?

4. How can we *teach* love in our church?

Conclusion

I hope that this study of Paul's theology and its implications has led us to a richer and broader understanding of the church's teaching ministry.

Certainly our study suggests that the church's educational ministry cannot be confined to the church school, or directed only toward children, or led only by a small group of teachers and officers. Rightly understood, the church's whole ministry is a ministry of teaching.

The church is the community which lives in the New Age. Its great responsibility is to recruit citizens for that New Age and to train those citizens to live responsibly. That task of recruitment and training is the heart of the church's ministry; and so the whole church is called to join in that ministry. To be sure, different ones of us minister in different ways, according to our gifts; but all of us plan and minister together.

The means by which the church recruits and trains citizens are as diverse as the diversity of the church's life. The whole ministry of proclamation, preaching, worship, witnessing is part of our educational task. Telling, acting out, and remembering the biblical stories and the other great stories of our tradition are part of our educational task. Thinking together responsibly about our ethical obligations and encouraging one another in the hard decisions which are required of Christian people are part of our educational task. The very business of seeking to live as Christian people, imitating—however poorly—Paul's zeal and Paul's commitment, is part of our educational task.

The church's whole ministry is a ministry of teaching because what we are called to teach are those great realities which are the signs of the New Age and the marks of the church's life: faith and love. Everything we do as a church is directed toward encouraging people to hear the word of God's love through faith and to turn to the neighbor and the world in love. Therefore, everything we do, rightly understood, is part of our teaching ministry.

Not only does the church teach by everything it does, but the church also teaches by what it is. Indeed, if one conviction has emerged from this study, it is this: the church best teaches by being the church. The church best teaches faith by being faithful. The church best teaches faith when it relies, not on its own striving, but on the free gift of God's mercy. The church best teaches love by being loving. The church best teaches love when its members are free to turn to one another in understanding and heartfelt concern. The church best teaches love when it is free to turn to the world in compassion and moral insight.

The church best teaches citizenship in the New Age when it really is the community of the New Age. When we live as the community without credentials, we teach that kind of faith which knows that it is by God's grace and not by our achievements that our lives are made rich and full. When we live as the community without distinctions, we teach that kind of love which takes no pride in its own gifts and feels no jealousy at another's gifts. We teach that kind of love which knows that when one of us is honored, we all rejoice. When one of us suffers, we all hurt. When we live as the community without end, we teach that kind of hope which sustains us in the face of an uncertain future for our world and certain death for ourselves and those we love. We live as those who confidently trust that "whether we live or whether we die, we are the Lord's" (Romans 14:8). When the church is what it is—the community of faith, hope, and love—then the church best teaches faith, hope, and love.

In teaching faith, hope, and love, however, the church does not teach about itself. The church teaches Jesus Christ. The church teaches Jesus Christ as the one in whom God declares God's good favor, which we receive by faith. The church teaches Jesus Christ as the one who has conquered death and futility and who therefore gives us hope for our lives and for human history. The church teaches Jesus Christ as the one who frees us to love and who shows forth the shape of love in his own life. The teaching church is never called to proclaim itself. In all it does and is, the teaching church proclaims Jesus, God's Chosen One, Lord of the church's life and of the new creation.

Notes

Chapter 1

[1] For good summaries of this history, see John Bright, *A History of Israel* (Philadelphia: The Westminster Press, 1959), pp. 341-412; and A. G. Wright, R. E. Murphy, and J. A. Fitzmyer, "A History of Israel," in *The Jerome Biblical Commentary,* ed. R. Brown et al. (Englewood Cliffs, N.J.: Prentice-Hall, Inc., 1968). vol. 2, pp. 689ff.

[2] For a good discussion of apocalyptic literature, see D. S. Russell, *The Method and Message of Jewish Apocalyptic* (Philadelphia: The Westminster Press, 1964).

[3] On the kingdom of God as a "symbol," see Norman Perrin, *Jesus and the Languages of the Kingdom* (Philadelphia: Fortress Press, 1975).

[4] This is a very brief summary of a good deal of recent literature on Jesus' teaching. See especially Rudolf Bultmann, *The History of the Synoptic Tradition,* trans. John Marsh (New York: Harper & Row, Publishers, 1963); Joachim Jeremias, *The Parables of Jesus,* trans. S. H. Hooke (New York: Charles Scribner's Sons, 1955); Norman Perrin, *Rediscovering the Teaching of Jesus* (New York: Harper & Row, Publishers, 1967).

[5] See W. D. Davies, *Introduction to Pharisaism* (Philadelphia: Fortress Press, 1967), p. 14; and *Paul and Rabbinic Judaism* (New York: Harper Torchbook, imprint of Harper & Row, Publishers, 1967), pp. 298ff.

[6] I am indebted to Richard Sammer for his help with this illustration.

Chapter 2

[1] See Ernst Käsemann, *Perspectives on Paul,* trans. Margaret Kohl (Philadelphia: Fortress Press, 1971), p. 103.

[2] This is not to say that 1 Corinthians 15 refers only to the resurrection of the church as the body of Christ and not to the resurrection of the "spiritual" bodies of individual believers. However, there is a "solidarity" of relationship between the risen Lord and believers after death (cf. 1 Corinthians 15:22).

[3] Cf. Käsemann, *op. cit.,* pp. 102-104.

Chapter 3

[1] For a much fuller discussion of this phenomenon, especially as it relates to the miracle and resurrection stories in the New Testament, see my book, *Fact and Faith* (Valley Forge: Judson Press, 1975).

[2] Albert C. Outler, *The Christian Tradition and the Unity We Seek* (New York: Oxford University Press, Inc., 1957), p. 141.

[3] We will have more to say about hearing and faith in chapter 4.

[4] I am indebted for this insight, in somewhat different form, to my teacher Nils Dahl, who pointed out in a class discussion that Paul sometimes argues, not from specifically Christian principles, but from common human understanding of what is right and useful.

[5] For an excellent study of the pattern of suffering and triumph as the imitation of Christ in Paul's ministry, cf. John Schütz, *Paul and the Anatomy of Apostolic Authority* (New York: Cambridge University Press, 1975).

Chapter 4

[1] See chapter 1, pp. 24-25.

[2] On this whole relationship of sin, pride, and the law, see Rudolf Bultmann, *Theology of the New Testament,* trans. Kendrick Grobel (New York: Charles Scribner's Sons, 1954), vol. 1, pp. 239-246. Much of this chapter is indebted to Bultmann's insights.

[3] See further our discussion of this point as it applies to our concern for godliness, chapter 1, pp. 24-27.

[4] Rudolf Bultmann, *op. cit.,* pp. 314-317, convincingly shows that obedience is one aspect of faith for Paul. He is less convincing when he argues that "Paul understands faith primarily as obedience" (p. 314).

[5] See also 2 Corinthians 10 and Bultmann's discussion of it in *Theology of the New Testament,* vol. 2, p. 315.

Chapter 5

[1] See chapter 2, pp. 38-40.

Suggested
Bibliography

Bornkamm, Gunther, *Paul.* Translated by D. M. G. Stalker. New York: Harper & Row, Publishers, 1971.

Bultmann, Rudolf, *Theology of the New Testament.* Translated by Kendrick Grobel. New York: Charles Scribner's Sons, 1954. Vol. 1, pp. 187-352.

Dahl, Nils A., "Anamnesis: Memory and Commemoration in Early Christianity," in *Jesus in the Memory of the Early Church.* Minneapolis: Augsburg Publishing House, 1976. Pp. 11-29.

_____, "Rudolf Bultmann's *Theology of the New Testament,*" in *The Crucified Messiah.* Minneapolis: Augsburg Publishing House, 1975. Pp. 90-128.

Davies, W. D., *Paul and Rabbinic Judaism.* New York: Harper & Row, Publishers, Harper Torchbooks, 1967.

Furnish, Victor Paul, *Theology and Ethics in Paul.* Nashville: Abingdon Press, 1968.

137

Käsemann, Ernst, *Perspectives on Paul*. Translated by Margaret Kohl. Philadelphia: Fortress Press, 1971.

Meeks, Wayne A., ed., *The Writings of St. Paul*. New York: W. W. Norton & Company, Inc., Norton Critical Edition Series, 1972.

Munck, Johannes, *Paul and the Salvation of Mankind*. Translated by Frank Clark. Atlanta: John Knox Press, 1959.

Nock, Arthur Darby, *St. Paul*. New York: Harper & Row, Publishers, Harper Torchbooks, 1948.

Roetzel, Calvin, *The Letters of Paul: Conversations in Context*. Atlanta: John Knox Press, 1975.

Rubenstein, Richard, *My Brother Paul*. New York: Harper & Row, Publishers, 1975.

Scroggs, Robin, *Paul for a New Day*. Philadelphia: Fortress Press, 1977.

Index of
Scripture Passages